THE BATTLE OF FINANCE AND FAME

A Financial Novel and Guide for Teenagers

Lisa McCorkle

ISBN: 978-1-7364451-0-5 (sc)
ISBN: 978-1-7364451-1-2 (e)

Library of Congress Control Number: 2020911650

CONTENTS

Preface vii

Acknowledgement ix

Chapter 1 Performing Over Budget 1

Chapter 2 Legacy 7

Chapter 3 Money Management 17

Chapter 4 Reality Or For Show 26

Chapter 5 Dream-Very High School 33

Chapter 6 Tracking Your Money 39

Chapter 7 Keep It 700 - FICO Score 50

Chapter 8 Battle Rap 58

Chapter 9 Authenticity 64

Chapter 10 The Nipsey Hussle 70

Chapter 11 Community Service 82

Chapter 12 Lose My Number! 92

Chapter 13 Integrity 109

Chapter 14 Managing Credit 114

Epilogue 132

Workbook: Teacher's Guide - Guided Reading Questions For Class Discussion 137

Understanding Chad's Credit Card Statement 140

PREFACE

Years ago, I became inspired to write this book because of the financial hardships I endured. I wanted to prevent others from having the same experiences.

Soon after landing my first job at the age of nineteen, the credit card companies came at me like vultures, enticing me to apply for credit cards. Of course, I started applying, and as expected, they granted me one.

Managing money wasn't taught during my years in school, and according to research, only a few states require students to take a high school course in personal finance, a necessary life skill. My knowledge of bank statements, interest fees, and credit cards was limited, to say the least. The single rule my mother taught me about credit cards was to pay my entire bill every month on time, and if I couldn't pay the entire bill, then at least I should pay three times the requested minimum amount. She believed that intentionally failing to repay a person or company, as promised, was stealing. She stood strong in that belief, which was exemplified through her excellent credit. She was a woman of integrity.

I followed her advice. But after a while, the shoes and clothes were calling out to me, and I started making exorbitant charges to my credit card, seeking instant gratification. It got to the point that my credit card bills exceeded my monthly net income. I was having a hard time trying to keep up with my monthly expenses, such as rent, utility bills, and car payment. I went from paying my credit card bills on time to paying them late or not at all, defaulting on my contract with the banks.

Determined to become a better manager of money, I committed myself to reading self-help books to obtain the skills needed to improve my finances and get out of debt. As I learned, I wanted to share my knowledge with others, particularly the younger generation. As a result, this concept was birthed, and I began working on this book.

Aspects of finance can be very intimating and boring; therefore, it was my mission to create an entertaining novel combining facts and fiction. The principles sketched in the book already exist; I'm simply making them accessible through an entertaining story that's practical, basic, relatable, and humorously woven together by relatable characters like Chad and his supporting cast as they navigate life in an ever- changing society.

I believe *The Battle of Finance and Fame* will inspire curiosity, imagination, and enjoyment for independent reading and learning. Most importantly, it will help readers make empowering choices and become assets to society. Enjoy reading *The Battle of Finance and Fame*.

ACKNOWLEDGEMENT

This book is dedicated to my Creator, family, friends, ancestors, and educators. Thank you for being positive influences in my life and believing in me. To the family members and my dear friends who were always excited about this book project from the moment I shared the idea with them many years ago. Their unwavering enthusiasm kept me on track.

Thanks to my parents: my dad, who will always remain my superhero; and my mom, who was my lead cheerleader. Their positive energy and spirit fueled my motivation to get it done. Their spirit surrounds me every day. A special thanks to my two children, Akiem and Wynter (a.k.a 2 Team), whose love makes me a better person. Last, but certainly not least, this book is dedicated to you, the reader.

CHAPTER 1

Performing Over Budget

"Yo, Chad. Get ready. You're up next."

The announcement sets Chad's nerves on edge. He feels the butterflies twirling around in the pit of his stomach. As he goes over his lines backstage, the anxiety chokes him, causing him to stumble over the words he repeatedly practiced before his bedroom mirror. This is the moment he's been anticipating. He has to be on his A game.

Chad is performing at the Villain Village. He's the opening act for KAVI-R, one of the heavy hitters in the rap game. Stepping back, he checks his reflection in the mirror. He spent his entire paycheck and borrowed money for his attire. The watch and the jewelry set him back $7,000. His white sneakers, trimmed in red and black, embroidered with a red hoop logo on the tongue and an air unit in the heel, cost $1,500, and his designer shades were $500. He knew he couldn't afford these things, and most of them were bought on credit, but he didn't care. If going broke was the sacrifice necessary to look the part, he felt it was worth it.

When the bill comes, I will deal with it later, he thinks. He starts going over his rap lines again. KAVI-R walks up to him and says, "This is your moment. Are you ready?"

"Yeah, I think so," Chad answers.

KAVI-R shakes his head and says, "Wrong answer! What do you mean, you think so? You have to know so!" Draping his arm around Chad in big-brotherly fashion, KAVI-R continues. "Listen up, if you want to be successful, there are two things I want you to remember. Number one, believe and have confidence in yourself. Don't doubt yourself, as others will start doubting you too. Don't empower other people's negative opinions by letting them feed off your self-esteem and deplete your identity.

"Be yourself, because you can't be anyone else. If you try to be something you're not, you won't last long in this business or any other business, for that matter.

"You're about to get signed to 4Real Dreams! This isn't a game. Which leads me to lesson number two." He pauses before continuing. "Success doesn't come overnight. You have to work hard to obtain it and, once achieved, work hard to *sustain* it. You have to be smart with your money. Invest your money and accumulate wealth. Protect what you gain. There are some hungry vultures in the world who will feed and starve you in one serving.

"Don't invest in expensive jewels, clothes, and cars just to look and act the part. Invest so that you actually become the part," he says with a grin.

A heart-to-heart from KAVI-R, a guy he has admired since forever, gasses up Chad's head. "Thanks ... and thanks for giving me this chance. I'm honored. You and the rappers before you wrote the blueprint for dudes like me. And that's real talk!" After a fist pound, KAVI-R walks off.

Chad is ready to become a megastar. He starts hopping around, bobbing and weaving, sticking and jabbing like he's about to do a few boxing rounds. His sparring match with the air comes to an abrupt halt when he hears the audience's chant. Chad listens intently, unsure whether he's hearing correctly. To his surprise, the crowd is calling his name. "Yo, those are my fans! And they're calling my name!" he says.

The thunderous sound of the fans chanting his name—"Chad ... Chad ... Chad"—gets louder, making him hyped. After the emcee makes an introduction, Chad appears, jogging around the circular stage, shouting, "What's up, New York?" over the blaring beats. The crowd goes bananas. The stadium reverberates. It's a pulsating energy.

"Vibe with me!" Standing in the middle of the stage, he zones out and starts dancing with the beat the DJ is cutting. After a minute or two, he opens up with his new song, "Servin' Luv 'n Da Club." The audience sings along with him.

Halfway into his set, Chad yells out, "Where my little stars at?"

"Ova here!" the crowd screams.

"I can't hear yaaaa! I said, where my little stars at?"

Girls are waving their hands in the air, shouting, "Ova here!"

The beat changes, and he goes into his second selection, "Twerk It, Twerk It, Little Star." Girls go wild. He looks into the crowd, not focusing on anyone or anything in particular. He can't make out any faces in the dimly lit arena. All he sees is a vast number of shadows encircling the stage, jumping up and down with electrifying energy; they are moving their bodies to the tempo. As he dances his way to the edge of the stage, he squats down to get closer to his fans. Sweaty bodies are smashed against the stage, shouting and pulling on him everywhere.

At that moment he decides to handpick a few females to join him onstage. One young lady in particular catches his eye, and he makes an attempt to get her onstage for a dance. It's futile, though, because out of nowhere comes another lady, who slithers her way in front and latches on to him, dragging him into the audience. *A little aggressive,* he thinks.

Security comes running, but Chad puts up his hand, signaling it's okay. Being in the middle of a huge crowd wasn't part of the plan, but Chad recovers quickly, keeps his cool, and continues to rap, paying close attention to the lady who pulled him in. Her alluring silhouette captures him. Barely able to see, he squints, studying her outfit. She's dressed in a black-sequined mini dress, which hugs her curvy body, and a sequined mask covering the top half of her face. The mask he finds a little strange but alluring and mysterious at the same time. The only thing Chad can make out are her sensual, sexy lips.

Momentarily mesmerized, he stares while rapping to the mystery lady. Taking her hand while holding the mic with the other, he draws her close, and together they dance, their moves feeding off each other, bodies in sync. In between verses, he whispers in her ear, "What's your name?"

Tilting her head back and staring into his eyes, she answers, "Ms. Fee."

Amused, he asks, "That's it? Is that your first or last name?"

She smiles seductively and says, "That's a conversation for later. For now that shall remain a mystery to you."

Not backing down from a challenge, he responds, "Not for long."

She gives him a half smile, which could mean a million things, but Chad doesn't care. While he keeps her engaged with his rap skills and impressive dance moves, his attention is diverted to a peculiar-looking gang a few feet behind her. They are fitted with white T-shirts emblazoned with black, three-digit numbers. They are noticeably standing out from the rest of the crowd. Their facial expressions are distorted, expressing a disinterest in his performance. The sight gives him an odd feeling.

The mystery lady who was dancing with him turns her back and drops it like it's hot. She smoothly dances her way over to the group with the embellished T-shirts. Chad, continuing with his performance, moves away, giving himself some distance, security following close behind.

Putting the peculiar lady and the group out of his mind, he focuses on the task at hand, giving the fans what they came to see. He continues rapping, mingling with the crowd, which is exploding with intense force. Everybody is feeling good and singing right along with him.

Suddenly, he notices the audience pointing in his direction. He turns around and finds the mystery lady seductively dancing behind him. He no longer feels the attraction, and his intuition communicates that something is off. But before he can figure it out, the white T-shirt gang surrounds him. Feeling a sense of danger, he makes his way back to the stage. Not realizing how far he has been swept into the crowd and away from security, he finds getting through the mob difficult.

As he makes his way back, the mystery lady sticks out her foot causing him to stumble. Holding on to the mic, he recovers. Again, the mystery lady covertly sticks out her foot, this time causing him to lose his balance. Chad finds himself looking up from the floor. At that moment, the DJ ceases the music, and Chad stops rapping.

Mayhem quickly follows. From a distance, security can be seen struggling to get through the sea of people, trying to prevent Chad from being trampled. The situation is chaotic as Chad tries to get his feet on solid ground. Finally standing, Chad can see the strange-looking gang prowling toward him. He tries to back up but is rooted in place, paralyzed by fear.

In one swift movement, they are in front of him, trying to grab the mic out of his hand, but he holds on tight, refusing to let go. Instincts kicking in, he turns around and makes a run for it. His first step is met with a thump on the back of his head. He becomes discombobulated.

"What the ...?"

From somewhere, the sound of security voices can be heard over the shouting fans. "Move! Move! Get out the way!" Their desperate efforts are slowed because of the commotion. The place is in total chaos. People are wildly running and falling everywhere.

The gang cages him in, taking his expensive watch, his shirt, even the expensive shades. "I can't believe they are robbing me," he says aloud.

One of them lunges into a rant. "This doesn't belong to you! You didn't work for this. You just wanna floss." Two of them bend down, grabbing hold of his ankles. They are feverishly trying to loosen his sneaker laces.

Oh no! Not the kicks! Mustering a little fight after the strike to the head, he swings, hitting one in the mouth with the mic.

They all move in, tackling him to the ground. From Chad's peripheral vision, a few feet away, he notices a tall man dressed in an impeccable gray suit urgently looking around. In that quick second, their eyes meet. He stares at Chad as if penetrating his soul. There is something familiar about him, Chad thinks.

With a few people separating them, the man makes an effort to reach out his hand, urging Chad to take it. Chad continues to fight back, trying his best to ward off the attack. Still the man urges Chad to take his hand. Chad wants to, but is reluctant to lose his grip on the mic. He continues to hold the mic tightly in one hand while trying to fight back with the other. The gang grabs and shakes him. With the mic still firmly in hand, he gets in a fetal position, trying to protect his face. They continue to shake him and are now calling his name. "Chad … Chad …"

He doesn't have a chance. He feels himself slipping away. With minimal strength, he pulls the mic to his lips and yells, "Help!"

CHAPTER 2

Legacy

"Chad! Chad, don't you hear me calling you, boy? Get up. Breakfast is almost ready," calls Poppa P, his grandfather.

Chad shakes himself fully awake. His eyes pop open in surprise, like he's been chased by a ghost. He finds Poppa P hovering over him.

"What's wrong? Did you have a bad dream?" Poppa P asks.

You're wearing that morning breath like cologne, Chad thinks. "Yeah, a nightmare. It seemed so real. I'm glad you woke me up when you did."

"I'm glad too. What was your nightmare about?"

"I was on stage, rapping with KAVI-R."

"Rapping?" Poppa P asks. "Yeah, that was a nightmare because … I got a rhyme for you. You can't rap for crap."

And you can't dress. Your shirt's lookin' like Grandma's old kitchen curtains. I wish somebody was bold enough to tell you to your face, Chad thinks.

"In your sleep, you were talking about 'Twerk It Twerk It Little Star.' Isn't that a nursery rhyme?" Poppa P is outspoken and speaks *his* truth whether you ask for it or not.

Chad sleepily stares at Poppa P, seeing the love behind the grumpy exterior. Poppa P is usually supportive. However, he refuses to be supportive of Chad's pursuit of rapping. "Your nightmare was trying to tell you something. Put down the mic and leave that rappin' stuff for legends like Snoop Dogg," Poppa P says in a concerned tone.

Boogalicious, the family's toy dog, jumps on the bed, fanning his off-white and apricot tail sixty miles a minute. His matte black button nose sniffs under Chad's chin. While Chad yawns, Boogalicious eases his round, fuzzy face upward, trying to sneak a lick on the mouth, vying for attention.

Chad jerks back, sideswiping the lip contact and pushing the dog to the side. "Move! Your breath stinks." Boogalicious sits, staring at Chad with his big, brown, sad eyes.

Poppa P shoos the dog off the bed. "Come on downstairs before your grandmother starts yelling for you. You know how she feels about her Saturday breakfast ritual, and forget about that rapping stuff. You can be many things, Son, but a rapper isn't one of them." He turns to walk out the door. "Talking about rapping with KAVI-R, shoot ... I have a better chance rapping with him," he mutters.

Boogalicious is right on his heel. "*Arf, arf.*"

Every chance he gets, Chad stands in front of a mirror, brush in his hand, practicing lyrics. He loves hip-hop but mostly the rapper's lifestyle, good music and fast money. That is what he wants. He doesn't realize hip-hop moguls don't get rich overnight. They hustled and struggled to get where they are, dedicating their souls and time to the art, creating masterpieces. Chad sees hip-hop only as a world full of fast cars, nice clothes, pretty girls, and lots of money.

He wants a rich lifestyle without the labor. Little does he know, he has the same potential as the successful moguls he looks up to, but he is too blinded by the bling to see that his poetic side should be applied elsewhere. He wants instant gratification without exploring his true identity.

Chad sits on the edge of the bed, pondering his bad dream. Lately he's been having recurring nightmares, which started soon after summer began. He doesn't know why this is happening. His summer sleeps have been robbed of peace.

He mentions the nightmares to his girlfriend, Melissa, but she laughs showing no concern. Normally, he wouldn't be troubled by a bad dream, but these nightmares have him spooked. They're constant and always similar.

He slowly rises from the bed and makes his way to the bathroom.

Downstairs, his grandmother is preparing breakfast, a routine she loves. Saturday morning is the only time she gets to bond with her entire family. The rest of the days, everyone is too busy, so she holds them to Saturday-morning sit-downs at the table. Her number one rule is no cell phones allowed. Chad and his divorced parents, Nicole and Vincent, reside in his paternal grandparents', Poppa and Momma P's, two-family brownstone. Poppa and Momma P are separated too. Their family living arrangement is unique, but it works for them.

His grandparents have been living in the brownstone for over thirty years. The house is paid in full. They are both retired; Poppa P was a police officer, and Momma P was a bank teller. They both live comfortably off their investments, pension, and social security. Even though Poppa and Momma P are separated, they both refuse to move out or sell their half of the house. Their solution was that Momma P would stay in the downstairs, four-bedroom apartment she shares with Vincent, Nicole, and Chad; while Poppa P would occupy the upstairs, two-bedroom apartment. Chad loves this arrangement and uses it to his advantage; most of the time he stays in the upstairs apartment with his grandfather.

His grandparents have access to each other's apartments. They have a tendency to walk in on each other unannounced, which has caused a few uncomfortable moments. However, they aren't deterred by those times. They continue to barge in on each other's space, sometimes without uttering a simple hello. They both fake the expression of annoyance, but a blind person could see they secretly enjoy each other's company. They are always sitting at the kitchen table, piecing a puzzle together, a hobby they started years back. They say figuring out puzzles builds patience and, once completed, a sense of accomplishment.

Poppa P walks into the kitchen and sneaks a piece of bacon. Boogalicious is on his heel, following him around, running and hopping in between his legs, looking for crumbs. Poppa P looks down. "Move before I trip on you and turn you into a little throw rug." The dog scrambles over to Momma P by the stove. He sits at her feet, wagging his tail fast and furious.

"Could you please walk the dog?" she asks.

Poppa P stares at her as if she has two heads. "No. I didn't retire to be walking a dog no bigger than my feet. A dog named Boogalicious at that. Who names a dog Boogalicious anyway?"

"Me!" she snaps.

"Well, 'me' should walk him," Poppa P fires back.

Momma P pushes, "Oh, so you're not going to walk the dog, like I asked."

"What part of that 'no' didn't you understand?" Poppa P snaps before continuing. "I don't even like calling him Boogalicious in the house, so what makes you think I want to call him that in public? You should be ashamed of yourself for naming him that. I ought to call DPS on you."

"You mean CPS, child protective services, silly," Momma P corrects.

"No. I got your silly. I mean DPS," Poppa P says. "Dog protective services."

"Well, I guess you'll be eating breakfast elsewhere," Momma P snaps.

"Where's the leash?" Poppa P turns away without another word.

Poppa P is by the door, preparing to take the dog for a walk. He goes in the closet to retrieve his sneakers and Boogalicious's leash and harness. While squatting down to put the harness on Boogalicious's neck, he gets really close to his face and says, "When we're out walking, you better stick close by me, because I don't want to have to call out your name to get your attention." To get his point across, he slowly asks, pronouncing each word, "Do. You. Hear. Me?"

Boogalicious barks. "*Arf! Arf!*"

As soon as they set foot outside, the dog breaks away and takes off down the block. Poppa P shouts, too embarrassed to call him by his name, "Hey ... hey, come back here."

Boogalicious doesn't listen. As he gets closer to the corner, Poppa P panics, scared the dog may run in the street or around the corner. Without a second thought, he shouts, "Boogalicious! Boogalicious! Come back here!"

The dog runs around the corner and out of sight. Poppa P takes off after him, huffing and puffing around the corner, yelling "Boogalicious! Booga—" Midway up the block, he stops upon notice of peering eyes, some seemingly mocking. Tilting his head slightly, he notices Boogalicious, belly up and spread eagle, on the lap of his longtime neighbor Ms. Annie.

Ms. Annie rocks in her chair, while rubbing the dog's belly. She smiles and waves at Poppa P with her free hand. He waves back and diverts his attention to the other early-bird ladies sitting on their porches, drinking coffee. One of them is wearing green leopard cat-shaped glasses and a lopsided wig with specks of lint; everyone on the block calls her "the witch." She comments with a smirk, "Oh, how cute. You named your little dog Boogalicious."

Poppa P is humiliated, so instead of gathering him up from Mrs. Annie's lap, he turns around and walks back home. Alone.

The witch yells after him, "Nice shirt!"

"Nice wig!" he yells back.

Later in the morning, everyone is awake and gathered at the kitchen table, eating a breakfast of waffles, bacon, and scrambled eggs. Momma P hands an egg-white omelet to Nicole and notices Boogalicious's absence. She questions the family, and Poppa P, looking up from his plate, lips greasy from eating the last piece of bacon, admits what happened and where he left Boogalicious. Between smacking his lips and slurping his last drop of orange juice, he relays every detail.

He finishes the story with, "Before we left, I told him to stick close by me so I wouldn't have to shout out his name." He pauses. "Obviously he didn't listen. And that's why he's not here with us now, sharing this delicious breakfast. By the way, you put your foot in this. Breakfast is delicious!"

Everyone around the table stops eating and is alarmingly quiet. Momma P's facial expression articulates true annoyance. She shoots up from her seat. Everyone's head jerks back. With a stern, no-nonsense voice, she hollers, "Chad, go and get Boogalicious!"
"Why do I have to get him? Poppa P is the one who left him."

Nicole and Vincent stare at their only son like he's crazy, both thinking, *Did this boy just fall down and bump his head? We're about to be childless.*

"Boy, don't sass me. Go and get him before I leave *you* at Mrs. Annie's with this donkey of a grandfather you got." Nicole and Vincent still don't say a word, afraid they may get dumped off at Mrs. Annie's too.

Full and content, the family lounges around the table before preparing to start their day.

"School will be starting soon. Twelfth grade should be exciting. Do you have any colleges in mind?" Momma P lovingly asks.

"Yes," Chad lies, hoping she doesn't ask for names.

"Remember what I always tell you. 'A lazy mind is the villain's playground.'"

"Yes, I remember, Momma P." Chad remembers, but he's not a bit concerned with college. He started lying to his family about his interest in college as soon as summer began. They've been asking him about college for the past few months, and he generally responds with a misleading answer. Lately he's been lying about a lot of things, even to his dad about looking for a job. His concentration is on football, nice clothes, his girlfriend, and joining the hip-hop world.

Poppa P interjects, "I hope he goes to college. Because if that 'Twerk It Twerk It Little Star' nursery rhyme is any indication of his rapping ability, he's in bad shape."

"Don't step on his dream. Everybody has a little poetry in them," Momma P says.

"A dream?" he asks. "If that's what you want to call it. Sounds more like a nightmare. And yes, I agree, everybody does have a little poetry in them, but the 'Twerk It Twerk It Little Star' baby rhyme is taken already, if you ask me."

"Well, nobody asked you," Momma P snaps.

"Somebody gotta tell him the truth. You know I don't tiptoe in the tulips. I tell it like I see it. And what I see is a bright young man with no rapping talent," Poppa P says.

"How would you know? You know nothing about the hip-hop world," Momma P challenges.

Poppa P gives her a wide-eye stare. "I know enough to recognize no talent when I see it."

"Well, my grandbaby will figure it out soon enough," Momma P says. "Life is like a brand-new puzzle. You open the box and pour the pieces out. Little by little, you start putting the pieces together. The puzzle doesn't become complete overnight, but you feel absolutely confident that the puzzle will be completed in due time because you know the manufacturer enclosed all the pieces you need."

Chad stares at his family. Not wanting to be caught in a web of lies and tired of them speaking about him like he's not in the room, he jumps up to leave. "I'm out! Oh, and Poppa P, 'Twerk It, Twerk It, Little Star' isn't a nursery rhyme. 'Twinkle, Twinkle, Little Star' is," he corrects. "And Mom, when you go to the mall later, don't forget about those sneakers I asked for. They came out today."

"I got you. I'll stop by Sneaker World later. But if I have to wait on a long wrap-around-a-corner line, you can forget it," she assures him.

Chad laughs, exiting the kitchen.

Vincent stares, annoyed, at Nicole and says, "He doesn't need anything else. I just bought him new clothes for school. Why are you buying him more?"

"Yeah, I know, but he's been asking me for those particular sneakers."

"How many particular sneakers does he need? And how many times do we have to have this conversation?" Vincent asks, thinking about the numerous arguments about her spending excessively on their son. It goes in one ear and out the other.

"As many times as you keep bringing it up," she responds smartly. "You submit to his every request. Nicole, he can't get everything he asks for. What part of that are you not getting?"

"I am entitled to buy whatever I feel he deserves," she says.

"Not if it's not earned."

Nicole inhales deeply before blowing out. "Listen, I don't have time for this. I'm sick of you telling me how I should spend my money."

"I'm not trying to tell you how you should spend your money. I'm just suggesting that you teach him the concept and value of money. Your way isn't teaching him productive habits that will benefit him later in life, like being responsible, having good work ethics, and developing money management skills. When was the last time you communicated your expectations of him or the consequences for not reaching those expectations?"

"Yeah, you may have a point," Nicole agrees, "but I say his time should be spent on attending school, doing homework, and studying. He doesn't have time for a job."

"Then we both need to sit down and teach him how to manage his time," Vincent says.

"Why should he have to work when he has parents who are more than capable of providing for his every need?" Nicole challenges.

"Didn't I just say to teach him the concept of money and responsibility?"

Nicole sighs. "I'm not having this same, tired conversation. I'm done. That's my baby, and I love him. I can buy whatever he wants."

She pushes her chair back from the table. Vincent does the same, preparing to exit, but not before saying, "You can't make up for lost time, Nicole. You're going to have to get a life of your own and find other ways to express your love toward our son. Love can't be bought."

The room becomes deafeningly quiet. Boogalicious jumps on Momma P's lap and buries his face in her cushiony body. Vincent squares his shoulders back, trying to pose in a confident stance.

Nicole stands, looking him square in the eyes, and asks, "Is that what you think?" She points at him. "You think I'm trying to make up for lost time."

Knowing this is a sensitive family subject they don't talk about anymore, but refusing to back down, Vincent says, "I don't think ... I know."

Too hurt to continue the conversation, Nicole says, "Later for you," while clearing the table.

Poppa and Momma P silently observe the heated exchange, whipping their heads back and forth from one to the other like they are watching a tennis match. "Who do you think will win?" Poppa P whispers.

"I don't know who'll win, but I know for sure who's going to lose if they don't come to some type of agreement," Momma P whispers back.

"Why are we whispering in our own house?" he asks aloud. "Listen, ya'll gonna stop all that fussing in here."

Nicole turns her attention to Poppa P. "Why are you down here? Aren't you supposed to be upstairs in your own apartment?"

"Listen here, little girl. Your good sense must be outside somewhere, keeping your hurt feelings company, because you sure done lost your mind. Asking me where I'm supposed to be? I *am* where I'm supposed to be—in *my* house. This is my house, the whole thing: the upstairs, the middle, the bottom, down to the tile you're standing on. You don't be questioning me like you're part owner. Don't get it crooked."

"You mean twisted, Pop," Vincent corrects.

"Yeah, whateva. You know what I mean—twisted, bent, not straight. It's all the same."

Poppa P continues, "Making all that noise about money. You young folks don't know how to save half a penny."

What's half of a penny? Vincent and Nicole think.

"Always looking for instant gratification," Poppa P continues.

"That's what I'm trying to tell her, Pop," Vincent interjects.

"Shut up and stop interrupting grown folks."

Nicole quietly snickers, feeling vindicated that Poppa P has shut Vincent down.

Poppa P ignores her. "Back in the day, your momma and I knew how to save a dollar. Despite many hardships and obstacles placed in our way, we fought, scraped, saved and creatively used our imagination to create a legacy for our offspring. Something of value, more than all that unnecessary material junk you buy." He looks at Nicole. "You folks are just leaving behind a bunch of debt for your children. You need to ask yourself, how can I use my money to pass on wisdom and value to my son?"

"How did we go from talking about Chad to *my* debt?" Nicole asks.

"Because, little girl, it's all related to personal finances. Your values are way off base. Before making financial decisions, ask yourself what purpose it will serve you and your son in the future. Measure your needs and know what it takes to provide for yourselves, your family, and your community. Teach your son to seek virtues of hard work and sacrifice, things that are meaningful and are long lasting that can be carried forward to future generations."

He gets up to walk out, but when he gets to the entrance, he turns back around and leaves them with these parting words. "Your greatest purpose in life should be about living a life of dignity and integrity and leaving an inheritance mixed with wisdom for your son." He walks out.

Nicole and Vincent stand there, staring at the empty spot Poppa P just occupied.

Vincent turns his head toward Nicole. "That was deep. I guess he told you," Vincent quips.

"I guess he told you too," Nicole fires back.

CHAPTER 3

Money Management

While walking to the train station, Chad ponders the new school year. The ringing of his cell phone interrupts his thoughts. After looking at the caller ID, he answers, "Yo, what's good?"

"My boy, CAP!" Jay, his best friend since the third grade, yells from the other end. Since they were little boys, Jay spent just about every weekend at Chad's. They were like brothers. Jay and a few others nicknamed Chad "CAP" from his initials.

"Where are you? I got some good news," Jay says.

"It must be good if you couldn't wait to tell me at school. I'm walking to the train station."

"Nah, it couldn't wait," Jay says excitedly. "I wanted to let you know about a rappin' competition that RETV is hosting."

Jason, known as Jay as everyone calls him, is also an aspiring rapper. He's talented at both writing and rapping. His ability to perform onstage is phenomenal, mirrored by the amount of trophies and money he's won. Jay is genuinely passionate about his artistry and will rap just for the love of rapping. When he performs, he lays his life—the good, the bad, and the ugly—at the audience's feet.

Jay didn't have a conventional upbringing and suffered from his family's financial state, leaving scars voiced through his lyrics. One of them is, "My family put the *D* in dysfunctional." Jay longs for the day of escape. In the meantime, he finds refuge in hip-hop. He's determined to make a good life for himself. He has an unwavering spirit that isn't going to allow the remnants of his past dictate his future.

His name was making a buzz in the battle-rap scene reaching the ears of a few well-known rappers, who owned their own label. Expressing himself in the most authentic way won him a lot of battles. If he was the rapper to go first, he would spill it all, including the tumultuous emotional and financial state his family was in, leaving no room for his opponents to diss him. He lyrically told his own story. When Jay was done, he eyed his opponent, pounded his chest, and said, "That's all me! Now, are you really who you claim to be?"

Jay is respected in the underground hip-hop arena for his skills and adored by the girls, who are attracted to his dirty-blond hair, blue eyes, and quiet spirit, which demands attention, sometimes unwanted attention. His handsome face, and stoic personality, offers an occasional smile that barely reaches his lips. People don't know what to make of him. Jay doesn't realize the magnitude of his presence; his demeanor works in his favor when he's competing in a rap battle.

Jay wants a girlfriend and a committed relationship, but for now he has one goal on his mind: saving enough money to make a video. To stay focused on reaching his dream, he's created a budget plan. His mother taught him how to manage money. He felt bad that she couldn't practice what she taught. They always found themselves in the dark due to his stepdad creating his *own* budget plan, which didn't include the light bill. His control over their household finances led to plenty of fights, and when the lights finally came back on, his mom was sometimes sporting a black eye.

Jay did his research and shopped around, finding someone who could produce his video for a reasonable price of $5,000. Every dollar from his wins goes into his student savings account for that purpose. He's already saved $2,000 from the rap competitions and $1,000 from his job at Burgerbun. He gets paid weekly, making ten dollars an hour. Each paycheck he grosses $250, but after deductions, his net income is $218.00.

Jay's Pay Stub

Employee: Jay	Required Deductions				
Earnings			Federal Income Tax	$00.00
Hours Worked: 25	**Rate per Hour: $10.00**	**This Period:** $250.00	FICA-Medicare	$6.08
Gross Pay		$250.00	State Income Tax	$00.00
			FICA-Social Security	$25.92
			Other Deductions	
			Health Insurance	$00.00
			Retirement Savings Account	$00.00
			Net Pay	$218.0

Each time he receives his check, he stares at the numbers, mean mugging the FICA and social security debits, and asking himself the same question every week. *Who are they? I'm sick of FICA and social security taking my money. I really need those extra dollars. I guess somebody else thinks they need it too.* Jay doesn't know he's going to need FICA, especially in his adult life. Right now, he isn't the least bit interested. Jay doesn't know that all employees pay into social security and Medicare, and that both programs are funded by FICA (Federal Insurance Contributions Act), which is a payroll tax; it is a required deduction his employer, Burgerbun, automatically takes out of his gross pay to cover contributions to social security and Medicare. If Jay understood, he would be happy to know that social security and Medicare act as a financial safety net to keep retired workers and some disabled people and their families out of poverty.

He creates a spending plan. It includes saving 10 percent of his net income for "just-in-case purposes," which he doesn't touch unless it's an extreme emergency. One of his mother's teachings he holds on to is, "To build wealth, always spend less than you make." He deposits $37.50 in his student savings account for his music video.

Jay's Four-Week Budget: $218.00 x 4 weeks = Monthly Budget = $872.00			
Description	Monthly Net Income after Taxes (+)	Expenses (-)	$ Available
Earnings-Burgerbun	$872.00		$872.00
Snack Money		$200.00	$672.00
"Just-in-Case" Funds		$88.00	$584.00
Savings for Music Video		$150.00	$434.00
Cell Phone		$125.00	$309.00
Entertainment/ Clothes		$300.00	$9.00

The remainder of his paycheck goes toward his cell phone bill, entertainment, clothes, and snacks. He eats at his job on most days, and on others he gets his grub on at Chad's. Momma P always has a home-cooked meal ready. He allots $300 for entertainment and clothing. Occasionally drawing on Chad's generosity, he has the fortune of applying that money to some other expense. Chad bestows Jay with clothes including items with never-removed tags, claiming they no longer fit. Jay knows that's Chad's way of looking out for him. Chad even gives his old Jordans away, but instead of wearing them, Jay sells them on eBay for more than what Chad paid for them. He advised Chad to do the same, but the response is always, "I don't have the patience for all that."

Each time Jay receives payment from a sale, it evokes another of his mother's teachings: "One man's trash is another man's treasure."

Jay continues, "The stakes are high. A few thousand in prize money. Two front-row tickets to a concert that everybody is talkin' about, and the winner will get to perform on the *Hip-Hop award show.* Oh wait! Some major players in the game are going to be there, and if they like your sound, they're giving the winner studio recording time, video included."

"Oh yeah! How much money you talkin' about?" Chad asks.

"I will text you all the details."

"Okay, cool. I'm about to go underground. I'll see you when I get to school."

When Chad enters the station's platform, he notices more than the usual amount of people. He sighs. *Must be a train delay.* The platform is mixed with a crowd of customers and station cleaners, who are fully clad in their blue uniforms, with the orange vests, and equipped with broom and dustpan.

A few minutes later, a train pulls into the station. Chad boards and takes a seat by the window, setting his book bag on the empty seat next to him. He reflects on his present life and imagines his future. He has a vivid imagination and uses it whenever he has time alone.

His thoughts about his future are interrupted by Addison, a special somebody he encountered at the beginning of summer at the movie theater. Sometime back, while sitting alone and waiting for the movie to start, Addison approached him unexpectedly. Chad was pleasantly surprised and welcomed the intrusion. It seems Addison came along just at the right time in Chad's life. Since the middle of eleventh grade, he's been at war with himself, stuck in between two worlds, often feeling guilty about not being honest with himself or his family. Addison has a peaceful way of connecting with him, trying to convince him that his insincere goals will never make him happy. The exchange of ideas is stimulating and compels him to think, which, for the most part, encourages him to dream about a successful future. In a short time, their relationship develops into something unique.

Addison exudes a calming essence, which appears to have the power to reveal the secrets of the soul.

Chad shifts his body, getting comfortable in his seat for the hour-long ride. As usual, Addison expresses a love for poetry, future goals, and unwavering plans to achieve them. Their discussion includes hip-hop, poetry, movies, and parties to social issues such as politics and money.

Looking down at his book bag spurs Chad to ask, "If you decide to go to college what will be your major?"

Addison considers the question thoughtfully. "Accounting."

Chad probes further. "Oh, so that's why you become so passionate when talking about numbers and money."

"I guess," says Addison.

"Maybe it would be an interesting college course." Chad hasn't made up his mind about attending college. He took the necessary tests and classes in the eleventh grade but only because they were expected. He's an average student who excels in math, his favorite subject. He has the potential of being accepted to a college, but his hopes and dreams are invested in becoming a rich rapper.

Curious about his response, Addison asks, "So you *are* thinking about going to college?"

Reluctantly, Chad answers, "Yeah," quickly changing the subject from college to rap. All summer he dedicated time for working on his rap lyrics, not once thinking about college.

"You want to be a rapper?" Addison asks, already knowing the answer.

"Yeah, you could say that ... I love their lifestyle."

"Are you interested in the *lifestyle* of hip-hop or the *art* of hip-hop?"

Chad hesitates for a moment, not sure how to answer. "The art of it."

Not convinced, Addison says, "Oh ... okay. If you say so."

Chad makes an attempt to divulge the nightmares he's been having lately. After some reservations, he decides to open up entirely, only because of Addison's nonjudgmental attitude. He goes into detail, while Addison listens intently. After Chad releases himself of the negative energy, a sense of relief takes its place. That is what he likes. Addison listens without judgment. Any internal fear he experiences is diminished with honesty and encouragement, traits he wishes his girlfriend, Melissa, had.

Addison probes, "How long have the nightmares been occurring?"

"For the entire summer," he answers.

"Don't you find it unusual that you are having the same nightmare repeatedly? Maybe it means something." Digging further, forcing him to think, Addison continues, "Did anything dramatic happen that you think activated these nightmares?"

"No, I had a good summer," he responds.

"Repeat the details of your dream again but keep them brief. We'll be getting off soon," Addison cautions.

Chad begins, "The first one started right after summer began. I was in Cali at my cousins'."

After Chad describes his first nightmare, Addison presses him for more details. "Okay, did something big happen on that particular day that you can remember?"

Chad sits there, thinking about that day, but nothing specific comes to mind. "Actually, it was a good day. My mom called me, excited about the promotion she got at her job. After talking about that, she switched the conversation to college and some other stuff. I told her I was excited about going. That was it. The most dramatic or exciting thing about that day was her promotion," he answers.

"You told your mom that you're excited about attending college. Are you *really*, or is your focus on becoming a rapper?"

Chad ponders the question.

Addison continues, "Perhaps you're not sure what you want to be. You say you want to be a rapper *and* a college student. It is possible to be both. However, is your heart truly in rapping *or* in school? Both or neither? You had a nightmare about college and another about performing on stage. Maybe it's showing you a struggle between the two because you're not being true to one or the other. When you mention you want to be a rapper, you say a *rich* rapper. Are you chasing the money or the true artistry? Maybe that's why the villains were taking your expensive clothes and jewelry while saying you didn't work for them, which could mean either two things: you didn't work for the clothes you had on, or you didn't work hard enough to be on stage performing."

"What? That's ludicrous." Chad retorts.

"Maybe. But give it some thought," Addison says.

"I just know the nightmares had me spooked," Chad says, before abruptly changing the subject to something pleasant for the remaining ride.

Money Management

1. List Jay's streams of income.
2. Why is it smart to keep a budget?
3. List a few things that should be included in a budget?
4. What was the last thing you bought?
   a. Why did you buy it?
   b. How did you get the money to buy it?
   c. Was the item you purchased a want or a need?
5. What is a written plan for spending the money you earn to cover your expenses?
6. An employee's paycheck before deductions is called gross income or net income?
7. An employee's paycheck after deductions is called gross income or net income?
8. What is the tax that pays for retirement and disability benefits?
9. What is the tax deducted from employees' paychecks that pays for medical benefits for people over sixty-five years of age?

CHAPTER 4

Reality or for Show

"OMG!" Melissa screams into the mirror. She leans in closer, taking inventory. A beautiful set of hazel eyes stares back at her. Water starts to form in her bottom eyelids. She blinks, desperately trying to prevent her tears from spilling over, but the more she stares at herself, the more futile the attempt becomes. Her vision becomes blurred as the tear gates release her shame.

As she watches, the tears roll between each pimple on her face. She says aloud, "My skin looks hideous." *Out of all the girls on the planet, why me? Why do I have to be the girl with bad acne? Why can't I have the perfect skin and body like the girls on Reality TV? I bet they don't have to go through this. They have an easy life.* She sniffles. Examining her face always sets off a flood of emotions and doubts.

Melissa's mind continues to wander. *That explains his sudden distracted behavior. I hope it's not another girl, one with smooth, clear skin; bigger breasts; and pouty lips.* Melissa pokes out her lips. *I wish I had fuller lips.* She places her hands under her breasts, lifting and squeezing them closer together.

Her thoughts are in overdrive. *Girls are always chasing after him. I can't blame them. He's tall and handsome with deep-set dimples. It better not be another girl, or it's going to be a problem,* she thinks while dropping her hands to her sides. Trying to wipe away all evidence of self-doubt, she rolls her eyes and, as a defense mechanism, plunges back into her usual moody attitude. It's a space where she feels safe and confident, a space that hides her inner turmoil. A space that covers her inner beauty and dominates her true identity.

Melissa's been dating Chad since the beginning of eleventh grade. They attend the same high school. Melissa has had a crush on him ever since seeing him rap in the cafeteria their sophomore year. He wants to be a famous rapper, and she wants to be the girl attached to somebody famous. She has hopes of being front and center with cameras rolling when Chad makes it big time. Her quest is to become a TV personality. For the entire summer break, she has been writing down ideas to pitch to anyone who will listen. She's always imagining a life with cameras following. Their claim to fame and fortune. *If others can claim their way to fame from that venue, so can I. I have a big personality too*, she thinks.

"Mel, hurry up out of that bathroom before you're late for school," Melissa's mother yells.

"Yo no voy a la escuela."

"What? Speak English or speaka de English," her mother annoyingly responds.

"I'm not feeling well. I don't think I can go to school today."

"You aren't missing the first day of school. So put a move on."

Melissa loves her mother, but this morning after looking in the mirror, she's not in a loving mood. She stayed up late the night before, trying to doctor the pimples sprinkled on her face. But the effort was useless. Everything she tried made them worse. She finally gave up after the dermatologist's and her mom's advice came to mind. *"You have to be patient, put your cream on, and give it time to work."*

I'm tired of hearing that, she tells herself. *When one bump leaves, three come back*. Blanketing her insecurities with a hot-pink fluffy towel, Melissa drags herself out of the bathroom, dreading school and hating her mother for making her go. She walks down the hall, glancing over the pictures hanging on the wall. Her eyes rest on one in particular, a family photo with her sitting in between her parents: her dad, Jose; and her mom, Tanya. Her heart softens as she wishes her parents were still together. But even though they're not, her dad spends time with her as much as possible. Her father is Puerto Rican, and her mother is African American. Melissa has the best of both worlds because it includes a wealth of culture from both parents. Living with her mother doesn't prevent her from being heavily involved with her Hispanic culture, thanks to her hands-on dad and Melissa's paternal grandmother.

She crosses her bedroom and tries to open her closet door, but it's stuck. She yanks the door open and is faced with a closet full of clothes and footwear. It's surprising that she can find anything in it. Looking through mounds of clothes, she decides on a pair of jeans and designer sneakers.

As usual, it's hard to find a shirt to hide the size of her chest. Melissa is extremely self-conscious about her small breast size and chooses clothes that hopefully will redirect attention from what she thinks is lacking in the cleavage department. Deciding to wear a brand-new white shirt, she readies herself, returning her thoughts to Chad. While Melissa is in her bedroom, covering her insecurities with designer clothes and lip gloss, and trying to figure out Chad's sudden change in behavior, her mom waits for her in her own room.

Tanya is across the hall, showered, dressed and ready to start her day at Bloomie's department store. She likes her job; it affords her the latest fashions due to her employee discount. She works there as a sales rep and makeup artist. She has always dreamed of owning her own makeup studio, but somewhere along the way, her dreams became buried under the burden of accumulated financial debt. Her dreams are now a distant memory. Tanya relaxes across her king-size bed. Her bedroom is an enclave of splendor, decorated and furnished with the best of everything. Her bedroom, just like her wardrobe, represents wealth, but her bank account exemplifies something totally different. She can't figure out how her financial life got so out of control. Maybe she knows the answer but chooses to keep it buried next to her dreams. She sits on the bed, holding the bills due this month and deciding which ones to pay first. She sighs, knowing the long hours she will have to work to pay them.

Melissa enters the kitchen, fully dressed. She grabs a box of cereal from atop the refrigerator. Retrieving a bowl from the cabinet, she sits down at the table to eat her breakfast and calls Chad. He doesn't answer, it goes straight to voice mail. *What's up with that?* Slowly chewing, she ponders who will be her teachers for the year, hoping they're not boring. *Maybe Chad finds me boring.* Melissa's thoughts are interrupted.

Tanya walks into the kitchen, looking like she just stepped out of a magazine. Designer labels are splayed across her body.

"How do you feel now that you're starting the twelfth grade?"

"La misma que la del año pasado."

"What?"

Melissa lets out a loud sigh. "Mom, please learn to speak Spanish. I said, 'The same as last year.' You look nice."

"Drop that sassy attitude and make sure you hit those books, more so than last year. And thank you." She pauses, giving Melissa a threatening look. "You have to buckle down and start preparing for college. I mean it."

Why isn't Chad answering my calls? Half ignoring her mother, she says, "Mom, if you had a lot of money, would you allow me to have plastic surgery?"

"No," her mom says and raises her eyebrows. "Even though you *act* ugly at times, you are beautiful just the way you are."

"But a lot of teenagers have procedures done."

"That's their business. Stop chasing their reality and create your own. You aren't a lot of teenagers, and I am *not* a lot of parents. Besides, what do you think needs to be enhanced?"

"If I told you, would you allow me to get it?" she probes.

"No."

"So what's the point in telling you?"

"Because I'm interested in your thoughts."

Melissa blows out hot air. "For one I would get something done about my hideous acne, and for another, I would get breast implants. I hate my little chest."

Tanya looks at her daughter compassionately, feeling her pain because she also has her own insecurities. "It seems like the more you watch those TV programs, the more dissatisfied you become with yourself. But there's an easy solution for the bad acne." Tanya pauses, giving Melissa time to reflect on her words.

Oh boy, here we go again, Melissa thinks.

"If you replaced sugary drinks with eight glasses of water a day, changed your eating habits to healthier foods like vegetables, and replaced high-fructose snacks with fruits like I've been telling you, the acne wouldn't exist."

"Ma, nobody wants a salad smoothie for breakfast, a spinach sandwich for lunch, and a broccoli Popsicle for a snack."

"They say it takes twenty-one days to break a habit. If you give yourself just that and leave all sugar alone, I guarantee that you can retrain your taste buds to crave veggies and fruits."

Vegetable nerd, maybe you're on to something. Look at your flawless skin. You could pass for one of the students in my school, Melissa thinks while staring at her mother's skin.

"I keep all this stuff in the fridge. It's there for you. You choose not to eat it." Tanya pauses. "As for your chest size, stand tall and be proud of your body. Love and respect your body, and your body will love and respect you back. That's all you have to be concerned about. Don't let anyone define what you should look like. There isn't one single person in this entire world fit to define you. Do you know why?"

Of course you can say that. You're beautiful with two nice cannon balls protruding from your blouse. "No, why?" Melissa asks.

"Because they, too, have a whole host of insecurities of their own. Trust me, everyone feels insecure about something. People just hide it in different ways."

"You're pretty. Mom, do you have insecurities?"

"Of course I do," Tanya answers. "I do the best I can with what I have and keep on moving. Do they get me down sometimes? Yes, I have my moments. I'm human. But I try my best not to let them get the best of me, and if they do, I shake them off. And if they're too much to shake off by myself, I call up my BFF, and we shake them off together. That always helps." She smiles before continuing. "The most important opinion that should count is yours. You have to be satisfied with your appearance despite other people's limited perceptions. That is how you build self-esteem—by not caring about others' opinions. Theirs should not matter over yours."

Whaa whaa whaa, blah blah blah. "Anywho. Would Dad give me the money?" Melissa quips.

Exasperated, Tanya says, "Really, Mel! Did anything I just say register?"

Melissa sucks her teeth. "*Vida apesta.*" Melissa's mother doesn't know how deep rooted this issue is for her daughter and that it will take a few more conversations to convince Melissa to embrace her already-beautiful body, mind, and spirit.

"We will talk about this later when I get home from work."

"Yeah, okay," Melissa says nonchalantly. "I'll probably be asleep by the time you get in." *Who are you fooling ... with the long hours you work? I'm glad I got the company of reality TV, my phone, and magazines to keep me company.*

Her mother winces. "Would you like a ride to school?"

"No, Dad is picking me up this morning." On cue the doorbell rings. Melissa greets her dad with a hug and kiss, his affection temporarily melting all anxieties.

Minutes later, Tanya walks out of the kitchen with her bag, car keys, and a sealed, stamped envelope in her hand. To Jose's amazement, it looks like a bill payment. Tanya's handling her financial business is a shock to him. He comments, "About time you're paying the creditors."

"I'm not paying them anything."

"Then what's in the envelope?"

"The same credit card bill they sent me."

Jose gives her an incredulous look. "You have the audacity to be *returning* the credit card statement. You're kidding, right?"

Tanya looks him dead in the eyes. "Look at me carefully. Does it look like I'm kidding?"

"The money you spent on the stamp could've gone toward your bill. Eso es el verdadero ignorante," Jose says.

"I caught the word *ignorant*. I will reopen this envelope if you have a check you would like to slide in; if you don't, I suggest you mind your own business, by taking Melissa to school."

Melissa watches the exchange, laughing aloud over her mother's antics. "That's funny."

Seeing his daughter laugh infuriates Jose. He doesn't find Tanya's pranks a bit funny, especially since she's their daughter's role model. Peering at Tanya, he says, "You think that's funny, but when all is said and done, the late fees you're going to accumulate will have you paying ten times over … like, forever. And whatever you bought will be worth zilch."

As he tells Melissa to get her things, Tanya stops her in her tracks. "Wait a minute, young lady. Go back in the kitchen and wash those dishes you left in the sink." Melissa gives her mother a you've-got-to-be-kidding look and says in a sing-song voice, "Dannnnng, its only two pieces."

"Good. You can count. Now make it zero," Tanya says in a do-not- make-me-have-to-tell-you-again kind of voice. As Tanya heads out the door, she kisses Melissa on the forehead and wishes her a great first day at school.

CHAPTER 5

Dream–Very High School

The redbrick high school is full of students and teachers all bustling around in preparation for the first day. You can feel the excitement in the air. It's easy to distinguish the student's grade levels. The seniors walk around self-assured like they own the school. They are the leaders. They feel like young adults, knowing this is their last year and the year in which their academic, educational, and personal goals should be set. Some will choose to go to college, while others will feel they aren't ready for the college experience and may decide to take some time off to reassess what they want out of life. Some will want to go to a trade school or work to earn some money, while others may feel propelled to join the armed services. Whatever they decide will be a new and exciting journey.

The juniors are excited about being one year away from becoming a senior. This is the year they register to take the PSAT in October, work hard to improve grades, prepare and review for the regent exams, and meet with their guidance counselors to review academic programs and graduation plans. Guidance counselors will discuss registering for the SAT in May or June. Hopefully most juniors have family members they can talk to about college prep programs available during the summer and about their college plans, tuition, and how everything will be financed.

The sophomores are glad they are no longer freshmen. Their once-perplexed looks have been replaced by mocking stares. Their attitudes toward the freshmen state, "I'm not a freshman, but you are." A few students have set new goals for this year. In a few months, they will be trickling down to the guidance counselor's office to discuss their academic classes and the PSAT; and to get help in preparation for their regents' exams. Many of them will expand their extracurricular activities list and start volunteering in school and the community.

Some of the freshmen can be spotted a mile away with their mystified looks while they search for a place to fit in. Some feel privileged because they already found a place with an upperclassman they knew beforehand. Like the upperclassmen, they will meet with their guidance counselors to review their classes and graduation requirements, set personal and educational goals for the year, create an academic and extracurricular portfolio, and participate in school and community activities.

In the midst of the mayhem, Melissa talks with her girlfriends by the trophy case. Some reveal who they hope to have as teachers, while others stake their claims on the boys they like. Of course, Melissa makes it known that Chad is off limits. Two bolder girls roll their eyes. *Who made her the spokesperson for this group?*

Melissa is actually the group leader. It's not certain how that title was delegated to her. It could be the way she took control of everything, her bold mouth or just her confident persona drawing other girls to her. Whatever the reason, it gave her the clout to pick and choose who she wants in her clique. In the middle of everyone talking, Melissa abruptly walks off, leaving the girls staring after her in wonderment.

"Chad ... Chad!" she calls through the crowd. Chad's tall, athletic frame with the afro Mohawk on top is hard to miss. He slows his pace and turns around, preparing himself for what he knows is coming next.

"Why didn't you answer my call this morning?" she says. "I called you twice."

"I don't know. I guess I didn't hear the phone."

She stares at him, agitated and definitely unconvinced. "Listen, I don't know what's up with you, but if you don't want to be bothered, just come out and say so."

"It's not that. I've just been busy."

"Yeah, it seems like all of a sudden something has your attention, and it's not me," she says with attitude.

"Yeah, it's some family stuff I'm dealing with," he lies.

Melissa softens a bit. "Why didn't you say so? You know you can talk to me. You used to talk to me all the time about everything. Lately, it seems as if you've changed."

Chad *is* changing. He feels it but doesn't understand it yet. Internally, he's struggling.

"So, what's on your mind," she pries.

He looks at her, almost as if second-guessing himself, then recaps his latest nightmare. After he's done, she stares at him.

"That was just a bad dream. And please don't tell me you're scared of a little ole boogeyman," she brushes him off with a laugh.

He stands there, feeling stupid for even telling her. *Addison never makes me feel silly*, he thinks.

"But I do like the part about you rapping on stage. I hope I was in the VIP section." Melissa smiles.

That's all you think about. Annoyed by her lack of concern, he dismisses himself by saying, "I have to get to class. I'm out."

"Will I see you after school?" she asks.

"I don't know," he says, walking off.

"Jeez, what's his problem?" Melissa says dramatically, looking around as if posing for cameras from her imaginary reality TV show. Then she walks back over to her friends to pretend everything is okay in her and Chad's world.

Chilled from the brisk autumn air, Melissa exits the train station, body digging into her jacket for warmth. Rain comes down in buckets, spraying wildly with the gusting winds. She gives up all hope of trying to keep shelter under her tattered umbrella. It's futile. The wind has torn it to shreds. She throws it in the nearest trash can, which is filled with other ragged umbrellas.

Shivering, she picks up speed, counting down the minutes until she's in the warmth of her dad's apartment. Her time is split, each parent gets two weekends a month. It's been that way since her parents' separation. The arrangement works for her. She loves spending time with her dad and looks forward to his cooking.

By the time Melissa makes it to the building, her clothes are soaked, and she's chilled to the bone. Trudging off the elevator, the soles of her rubber boots squelching across the slippery floor, Melissa's ears are met with the sounds of salsa music coming from a neighbor's apartment. Momentarily forgetting her uncomfortable predicament, she's comforted that it's Friday, that her boyfriend is coming over, and that she will soon be enveloped in warm clothes. She gyrates her hips, making a puddle in front of the door, while she fishes for her keys. Swaying her hips, captured by the beat, she becomes temporarily deaf to everything around her and doesn't hear her name being called.

"Melissa! Melissa!" her dad's neighbor yells.

"Sí! I'm so sorry, I didn't hear you," Melissa responds, embarrassed.

The neighbor smiles, "Como está?"

"Muy bien," answers Melissa as the lock clicks and she opens the door to the apartment.

Immediately after entering, the great aroma of sofrito wafts through the air. Her nose captures the warm smell, and she feels as if she's died and gone to Goya heaven. Discarding her boots by the door, she follows the aroma, like a stalker, to the kitchen. She walks to the stove and lifts up lid after lid, gazing over at each delicious-looking dish. Her eyes are greeted with beautiful colors of orange, yellow, and specks of red.

Her dad enters the kitchen. "Hola, Melissa."

Melissa returns the greeting. "Hola, Papi," she says, accompanied by a kiss and a huge hug.

Chad arrives a few hours later. Together they eat dinner with her dad, who immediately retires to his bedroom after cleanup, making sure his door remains open. Full and content, Melissa and Chad lazily sprawl on the couch, watching a reality TV program. After much debate over what to watch, Chad gives up, too tired to protest.

"You know their boobs are fake, right?" Melissa points out halfway through the show. Chad looks up and refocuses his attention on the program.

"What?"

She repeats, "Their boobs ... they're not really that big. It's implants."

"Okay, and ..."

Feeling foolish, she says, "I'm just saying." She wants to make sure her boyfriend knows she isn't alone in the small-breast department. The only difference is that they have money to do something about it.

"You know how you guys are always talking to female body parts instead of the girl." Melissa looks pointedly at him.

"Just so you know, guys do have the capacity to think about things besides a female's body parts."

While Melissa is engrossed in the show, he is sitting there, thinking about starting a new job.

The week prior, he went to the movies alone because he didn't have enough money to purchase two tickets. At times, he likes being alone at the movie theater; it's where he finds solitude, where his thoughts become clearer. That day he had an unexpected encounter with Addison, who suggested he apply for a job at the theater. It was then that he decided that maybe it would be a good idea to work there. He applied for the job online and is now waiting to hear back from the manager.

He tells Melissa his plans, but her response isn't what he was expecting. It isn't encouraging. In fact, it seems as if she doesn't want him working at the theater.

"Why would you want a job there?" she asks.

You see, it's attitudes like this that turn me off. "What's wrong with working at the theater?"

"There's nothing wrong with working there, but ... I just expect you to be doing something better than that."

"Like what?" he asks impatiently. "I'm only a teenager with no work experience." *I know working at the theater doesn't fit your big dreams of becoming a TV personality.*

Melissa tries to talk him out of it knowing the job will impose on their time together. "I don't know. Shouldn't you be practicing for the upcoming rapping competition? I can't wait until we get on TV!"

I don't have the energy to try to change your mind. You wouldn't understand anyway. "Yeah, you're right."

They talk about his plan to join the hip-hop world, a topic that makes her hazel eyes light up with delight.

As the program changes to scenes for the next episode, Melissa becomes glum. *What do I care about big breasts and perfect skin? I can take a plunge in Chad's hip-hop world and have the stardom that will create the opportunity of a lifetime. I could become rich and famous in one shot.*

Chad and Melissa started dating a year ago. When they first got together, they were inseparable, spending most of their free time together. They had a lot in common. Chad had dreams of becoming a rich rapper, and Melissa had dreams of becoming the next successful TV personality. Their status as a couple in school put them in the position to be nominated the cutest couple in the yearbook. Their dreams aligned, and their mission was to be a wealthy power couple. But lately Chad's feelings have shifted, and he can't articulate them. It feels like a force is pulling him in another direction away from Melissa.

As the evening passes, Chad finds himself tired and bored. It's a feeling he never experienced in Melissa's company before. His desire to leave is strong. He gives in to it, fakes a yawn, and prepares to leave. As they say their goodbyes by the door, Melissa reminds Chad of their date the following weekend. He tells her that he remembers and gives her a kiss good night. She closes the door behind him.

CHAPTER 6

Tracking Your Money

"I don't have all day," snaps an impatient customer interrupting Chad from his daydream. The job Chad applied for finally called. His dad and grandparents are proud of him. They want him to develop strong work ethics, and learn how to manage an income.

His mother is proud but feels a tad bit sad. She thinks her baby boy is slipping away.

Chad's been working there for some time and looks forward to payday. He's adapting well to his new role but still trying to figure out how to deal with his uptight manager and rude customers. His manager is a strict, by-the- book, grim-faced kind of guy. The employees call him "The Gremlin" behind his back. A few of his co-workers tell Chad not to worry about him, just to be careful and watch his back. "He's quick to fire a person for any minor thing," they say. So between the manager and the customers, work takes almost every ounce of Chad's patience.

The lady continues, "The movie is about to start. I would like fries with cheese, a hot dog, and a medium Coke. How much is the soda?"

"Six fifty," Chad answers.

"What? Six fifty!" the lady shrieks.

Chad looks at the lady like she has two heads. "Uhh … yes." He's frustrated with customers acting crazy and taking it out on him when he tells them the prices.

"Why is it so high?"

"Miss, how old are you?"

"What?" the lady asks indignantly.

"No disrespect, but you look like a grown woman who's been going to the movies for a long time. The prices shouldn't be breaking news to you. I didn't create the prices. I just work here."

The lady stands there, looking dumbfounded. She knows he's right but is too embarrassed to admit it. "Just ring up my stuff so I can catch my movie."

The waiting patrons hear the exchange and let out a chuckle. Chad's co-workers enjoy his dry sense of humor and think he's funny, especially when dealing with some of the overbearing customers. What's even more comical to them is that his intention isn't to be funny.

His manager is off to the side, watching and taking notes; he doesn't find anything humorous about the exchange. As he scribbles notes in his pad, he makes a mental note to reprimand Chad for the incident. This isn't the first time Chad has been impatient with a customer. All employees are expected to be polite to customers despite their rude attitudes.

From his peripheral vision, Chad sees Melissa and one of her friends walk by. He glances over at her quickly before turning his attention back to the task at hand. Still ticked off by the loudmouthed customer, he begins to fill the order by picking out the most burned hotdog he can find.

"Why didn't you tell me you were coming here to see a movie?" Chad asks Melissa while on break. Melissa looks at him, trying to decide whether he is joking. *I wonder why he's surprised and not just happy to see me. Maybe it's time I start coming here unannounced more often.*

"I didn't know I had to tell you. Besides, this is the only time I get to see you nowadays." Before he can respond, she continues, "Since you started working, I barely see you unless we pass each other in the school halls. What time are you getting off? Maybe I can wait for you."

Not wanting to be hassled about his job or for not spending enough time with her, he says, "No, that's okay. I may do some extra hours."

She rolls her eyes. "Yeah, I figured. Well, anyway, let me go. The movie is about to start." Melissa has been suspicious of Chad's behavior for quite some time, and his response doesn't help matters; it only feeds her insecurities.

Apparently feeling bad, Chad says, "On my next day off, I promise you and I will do something together. I get paid this week."

"Yeah, okay," she says unenthusiastically while strutting off. She doesn't know how to handle Chad's recent lack of attention. Melissa's self-esteem relies on Chad's companionship. His company is her security blanket. In his presence, she forgets about her small breasts and less-than-flawless skin. In her and Chad's world, she is perfect.

At the end of Chad's shift, he waits in the manager's office for his paycheck, dreading the weekly hassle of cashing his check. Every pay week, he has to go to the check cashing store and wait thirty minutes on a line to cash his check for a fee. He's tired of the fees.

Chad heads home fed up with the fees they charge him for cashing his check, promising himself it will be the last time going to a check cashing store.

Taking Momma P's suggestion, Chad's mother opened a student account for him. He now has a savings and checking account.

She notes that the statement would come in both the guardian's and student's names: the student as the primary owner and the guardian as the secondary owner. She said it was a good way for Chad to create a financial history. At first his mother was reluctant, but after explaining that the account would be separate from the one that already existed, she relented. Momma P explained that the account would have no monthly service fee and that he could have direct deposit so his paycheck would go directly into his checking account.

He also could have his own debit card. She told him to withdraw money from his bank and not from automatic teller machine (ATMs) in other banks or convenience stores. Other businesses charge up to five dollars or more for using their ATMs. Chad feels it's ludicrous to be charged a fee to take out his own money.

Momma P goes even further and explains the meaning and importance of a bank statement, and how to keep track of each transaction. Now that he is working, Momma P wants to make sure her grandson is equipped with the tools he needs to handle his personal finances. She tells him that poor money behavior leads to a road of misery.

Sitting around the dinner table, Momma P has her financial papers spread out, explaining the meaning of her bank statement, and how she keeps track of her transactions through a spreadsheet.

Chad's parents and Poppa P joins them at the table helping themselves to dessert.

Poppa P leans in to listen.

"Now listen, baby. This here is my checking account statement. I'm going to show you how to review a bank statement and compare it to a spreadsheet that I want you to create for yourself." She looks up and sees Poppa P intently listening. "Don't you have someplace to be?"

"No," Poppa P quips.

"Well, I'm teaching our grandson how to manage money, so keep quiet and don't say a word."

Poppa P looks around and says, "You must be talking to one of them because I know you're not talking to me."

Ignoring him and returning her attention to Chad, she continues, "So this right here is my bank statement, and the spreadsheet I created for myself."

Bank Statement

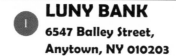

LUNY BANK
**6547 Balley Street,
Anytown, NY 010203**

Momma Pratt
1234 Your Street
Brooklyn, NY 00000

Checking Account Number: 234321654

This statement shows transactions for the period of December 1, to December 31,

Activity Summary
Deposits (+): $2000.00
Misc. Debits (1420.51)
Fees (-): 0.00
Ending Balance: $729.49

Date	Description	Deposit (Money In)	Withdrawal (Money Out)	Account Balance
	Beginning Balance			$150.00
12-5	Deposit	2000.00		2150.00
12-6	Gas		40.00	2110.00
12-6	Bank Withdrawal		60.00	2050.00
12-19	Diner		120.00	1930.00
12-20	Light Payment		178.00	1752.00
12-20	Lingerie Store		350.00	1402.00
12-22	Cell Phone		89.97	1312.03
12-27	FoodMart		582.54	729.49

Thanks for banking with us. Our Customer Service Number is 1-800-000-0000

1. Bank Name: The name of your institution and its address.
2. Personal Information: Your full name and permanent address. If you have plans to move, make sure to let the bank know so they can send your statements accordingly.
3. Account Information: The type of account and the account number
4. Statement Period: The dates the statement covers
5. Activity Summary: An overview of your deposits, withdrawals, and service fees as well as the balance remaining at the end of the period. On your statement, you will be able to note any fees you've incurred. These will be deducted from your monthly balance. If you overdraw your account, you will need to pay this money back to the bank, along with any other interest and charges. By paying attention to this section of the statement, you will become aware of miscellaneous bank fees you're being charged and thus take appropriate action to avoid incurring them in the future.
6. Transaction Summary: A detailed listing of your credits and debits. It shows the date (transaction date), description (where and whom the transaction took place with), deposits (money put into the account), and withdrawals (money taken out or spent).

After reviewing the bank statement with Chad and explaining each line, Momma P shows the spreadsheet she created to keep track of each transaction and how the ending balance match her bank statement.

Spreadsheet:

Date	Description	Income Money In	Expense Money Out	Balance
12/5				150.00
12/5		2000.00		2150.00
12/6	Gas		40.00	2110.00
12/6	Bank Withdrawal		60.00	2050.00
12/19	Diner		120.00	1930.00
12/20	Light Payment		178.00	1752.00
12/20	Lingerie Store		350.00	1402.00
12/22	Cell Phone		89.97	1312.03
12/27	FoodMart		582.54	729.49

"Hold up! Wait one minute!" Poppa P interjects. "I see over here on December twentieth," he says, pointing to her spreadsheet, "that you spent three hundred fifty dollars on lingerie. For what?"

Momma P squints and says, "For none of your business. I already warned you to keep quiet while I'm trying to teach our grandson. You can go upstairs with that foolishness."

"If I have to go back upstairs, I'm taking my puzzle with me. You know, the puzzles you like to figure out with me." He winks and smiles. She rolls her eyes and continues to explain to Chad the importance of living within his means and not spending more than he can afford, imparting the vital lesson of living his life honestly.

Momma P wants Chad to fully understand the process. Even though a few of the things being taught aren't relevant at the moment, she knows they will be useful when financial circumstances arrive.

Momma P continues, "Even though I know everything these days is paid online or some other convenient way, it's still a good idea to create and use your own tracking method that works best for you. There are plenty of personal finance apps that is good for keeping track of your spending and helping to create a budget. Now that I gave you this information, you can never say you didn't know."

Poppa P interjects, "May I please say something to my grandson?" Not waiting for an answer, he continues, "I want you to remember that learning through other people and school aren't enough for personal growth. It must be combined with having life experience and honoring your instincts. Combine those together, and you will have a great financial life."

Momma P knows Chad had been given a lot of information in one setting and wants to lighten up the conversation. "So, how is your rapping coming along? Are you still practicing your lines for that rap competition?"

Before Chad can answer, Poppa P says, "Shoot, he has to find a verse first."

"My rap lines are going good," he answers.

"Boy! You need to stop that lying! I know you're not still talking about that 'Twerk It Twerk It Little Star' nursery rhyme. You know good and well that rapping isn't going nowhere. Not even a little bit." For a split second everything is quiet. The silence is broken with, "Oh shoot!" Poppa P points.

Everyone freezes, expecting the worst as they yell back, "What?!"

"Over there, between the fridge and the cabinet," Poppa P answers.

Momma P and Nicole knock each other over trying to stand on the same chair. Nicole gives up and jumps on a different one. Vincent walks to the refrigerator to investigate. Peering between the cabinet and fridge, he says, "What, Pop? I don't see anything."

"You don't see it?" Poppa P asks in a shocked voice. "Look good! Did you find it?"

"Find *what*?" Vincent repeats, exasperated.

"Chad's rap line." Poppa P laughs, and Vincent, who can't help it, joins in. The women get down from the chairs, rolling their eyes and sucking their teeth.

"I do have a few new rap verses," Chad says in his defense. Lately he hasn't actually been practicing or trying to come up with anything new or original. Poppa P stares at him pitifully, shaking his head. He adores and loves his only grandson; he just has an eccentric way of expressing it. He doesn't sugarcoat anything; he gets straight to the point.

His grandfather is hard on him only because he knows the truth and wants to make his grandson realize that. He knows Chad isn't seeking his true purpose. It's evident to him that Chad isn't really interested in becoming a rapper and isn't willing to put in the hard work, that he is fascinated only with the lifestyle.

"Then what is it? What are the new verses? Quieter minds want to know," Poppa P says.

"Inquiring minds!" everyone yells.

Chad's dad, too, isn't letting him off the hook. He says, "So go ahead, Son. Rap a few new lines for us." Chad sits there, quietly clueless.

"Exactly my point," Poppa P jokes. "When your mother goes to the mall today, ask her to stop in one of those stores and buy one for you. They may have a rap verse she can catch on sale. I bet they come in different colors. I heard green is the color this season."

Momma P rolls her eyes at her husband and says, "That's enough with the jokes."

"What eva," Poppa P says.

"Whatever!" they all yell.

Momma P continues, "But seriously, baby, if you want to be a rapper, that's fine as long as it's your purpose in life. Life without a purpose is a tragedy." She focuses on her grandson. "And what's even more tragic is when you discover your purpose but you're not willing to work hard and persistently to attain it. If rapping is something that drives you and it's truly your passion, I say go for it."

Momma P hardly takes a breath. "Life purpose is the reason you are here on this earth. Who you want to be and what you want to create—those choices will impact the world, including your family and community. And your question to yourself should be, 'What sacrifices am I making now to do that?'"

Lisa McCorkle

Key Points

You can establish credit by opening a savings or checking account and carefully managing it. Lots of teens have already started the process of establishing credit by opening savings and checking accounts. Nearly two out of every three teenagers of high school age have a savings accounts, and about one in five has a checking account.

Keep Track of Your Expenses

Review the blank spreadsheet. Fill it in to organize the following nine activities. Do the math yourself and record your new balance after each entry. When you are finished, compare your balance to the balance below. If your balance doesn't match, review your entries to see where you went wrong.

Date	Description	Income Money In	Expense Money Out	Balance

1. January 7: Your balance is $247.16.
2. January 10: You get a paycheck for January 1–10 in the

amount of $373.64 and deposit in your account.

3. February 4: It's your birthday! Your aunt gives you $50. You deposit it on that day.
4. February 5: You go to a concert and run out of money. You use the ATM in the lobby to get $25 for snacks. The ATM charged a $3.00 fee.
5. February 10: Your credit card bill is due on February 17, you pay your bill online in the amount of $41.16.
6. February 11: Your sister owes you money. She pays you $20. You deposit the money in your account.
7. February 13: You need to buy flowers for your grandmother's birthday. You go to the ATM at a convenience store and withdraw $25. The ATM charged a $5.00 fee.
8. February 16: You deposit your paycheck for February 1–15 in the amount of $182.43.
9. February 18: You take out $400.00 to put in your savings account.

The ending balance is $ 390.07.

CHAPTER 7

Keep it 700 ~ FICO Score

"Hey, I've noticed you haven't mentioned any of your nightmares lately," Melissa says while she and Chad walk to the train station on the way from a restaurant.

"Yeah ... come to think of it, I haven't," Chad says thoughtfully, just realizing it himself. Since he started his job, he hasn't had one. *Maybe it's because I've been busy.* Practicing for the competition has taken a backseat. Lately he's been consumed with working, saving money, attending school, and concentrating on college applications. "Actually, I wake up from my dreams with a smile on my face. Last week I had a dream I was a successful businessman. It wasn't quite clear, but I was dressed in a nice suit in an office, which seemed to be my office, helping a couple out with some financial stuff. Something that had to do with numbers. I think I owned the company because I remember people coming up to me and asking me to sign important papers."

Since his job started, Chad has been able to take Melissa out on more dates and is proud to use his credit card when paying for dinners. His mother opened up a secured credit card and added him as an authorized user. A secured credit card requires a deposit. She deposited $1,500 and told Chad it was totally his responsibility to pay his own monthly bill. She even drew up a written contract with a promise from him that he would pay the balance in full every month. She gave him the card because he proved to be more responsible since starting his job. He's been saving money and using his debit card maturely. She thinks it's an ideal opportunity to help him build positive financial behavior.

Momma P thought $1,500 was too much money to deposit and suggested $500 instead. Poppa P suggested zero. He was against the entire thing. Nicole didn't take heed, deciding to do what she thought best. The day she gave Chad the card, she explained that a secured card worked just like a credit card. The only difference was that a deposit was required to open the account, and his credit limit would be limited to the amount on deposit. His mother made sure the secured card reported his bill payment history to at least one credit bureau so Chad could start building a solid credit history for himself. She told him to make sure to keep track of every credit card purchase each month by reviewing his statements and ensuring their accuracy.

"Spend only as much as you can afford, or less, and don't use a credit card for purchases of less than ten dollars, because small purchases add up fast. Use cash instead." Chad's mother shows him how to go online to make sure there is nothing suspect or any unauthorized charges made on his credit card. She wants him to be aware of identity theft and lets him know it can occur when someone goes through records from his employer, hacks his computer, goes through his trash, or steals his mail or wallet. She tells him he can avoid identify theft by not giving out personal information, such as his social security number, mother's maiden name, or account numbers, over the phone or Internet unless he knows the information is secure. She sums up the conversation by telling him to keep his license, social security, and credit card numbers safe and private.

The real-life scenarios of compromised credit cards propel Chad to monitor his cards online three times a week.

"It's difficult to prove your innocence once your card has been damaged by an unauthorized user," Nicole tells him. "And the collection agencies! Boy, are they relentless. They will come after you like *hound dogs*," his mother says. The stories he hears are scary, especially the ones about the damage an unauthorized user can do to a person's FICO score.

She tells him the Fair Isaac Corporation created FICO scores and that they are a way of measuring an individual's creditworthiness based on a number of factors, like payment history, how long the person has had credit lines open, and whether the person is late on any accounts. His mother goes online at Myfico.com and gives him the breakdown of an individual's FICO score based on Fair Isaac's explanation.

- 35 percent depends on your payment history, including delinquencies and late payments.
- 30 percent depends on how much you owe and your debt-utilization ratio, which is how much you owe compared to your overall credit limit.
- 15 percent depends on the age of your accounts.
- 10 percent depends on new credit, a category that includes recent inquiries into your credit score, new accounts opened, and whether you had bad credit in the past but are working to turn it around.
- 10 percent depends on the types of credit you use: credit card debt, student loan debt, and so forth.

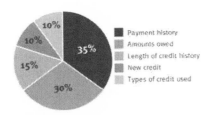

She also explains the numbers behind the FICO score, which range between 350 and 850. A score of 650 is considered "fair," while 750 or higher is considered "excellent." These scores determine and impact a person's renting and buying ability. She describes her experience and what she had to go through a few years ago when purchasing a car. She admits that the car she had was in Chad's father's name because of her poor credit score, and she describes the difference it made in her monthly payments. The bank was going to charge her

8.9 percent interest on her $15,000 car, so her monthly payment would have been $310.65, based on her FICO score of 620. She couldn't afford that payment, so she asked Chad's father to finance the car with a promise to faithfully pay him every month. His FICO score was above 750, so the bank charged him an interest rate of only 6.5 percent, decreasing the monthly payment to $262.85. She finishes the lesson by saying, "A FICO score is a convenient way to summarize an individual's credit history and is included in a credit report."

After Chad's mother tells him that a good FICO score of 700 or above will make it easier for him to rent an apartment, buy a house, purchase a car, start a business, get his own cell phone account, and do other things, his attitude instantly changes. The FICO score numbers will be forever implanted in his brain. His new mantra is, "Keeping it 700."

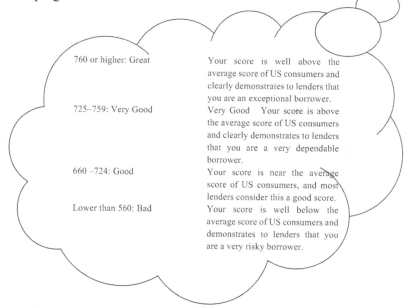

760 or higher: Great — Your score is well above the average score of US consumers and clearly demonstrates to lenders that you are an exceptional borrower.

725–759: Very Good — Very Good Your score is above the average score of US consumers and clearly demonstrates to lenders that you are a very dependable borrower.

660 –724: Good — Your score is near the average score of US consumers, and most lenders consider this a good score.

Lower than 560: Bad — Your score is well below the average score of US consumers and demonstrates to lenders that you are a very risky borrower.

Chad protects his card at all costs. He feels like a responsible person when handling his business; this makes him want to be a more responsible boyfriend. He makes an effort to spend more time with Melissa in between school and work.

The young couple is immensely enjoying their time together; both wanting to prolong the evening as it is slowly coming to an end.

Chad continues his earlier train of thought. "Addison was probably on to something. Since I started being more focused, I haven't had a nightmare."

"Addison ... who is Addison?"

Oops. How did I let that slip. Up until he became familiar with Addison, Chad has pretty much gone along with Melissa's ideas on a lot of things. He now finds himself questioning his actions. Melissa has been instrumental in persuading him to join the ranks of other aspiring rap artists for the competition, but he feels Addison, on the other hand, is the catalyst he needs right now. He rubs his hand over his head. "Oh, somebody who works at the theater," he lies.

"She must be more than some girl if you are telling her about your personal business. You're barely comfortable telling me."

That's because you always laugh it off. "It's not that personal. I just mentioned it in casual conversation."

He cuts his eye in her direction, imagining what she's thinking.

"You need to hurry up and get that car so we can stop riding the train," Melissa whines. "I'm tired of riding the train." Which tells him that the mention of Addison's name has now spoiled her mood.

"You weren't tired a few months ago," Chad says, totally annoyed by her comment. It's attitudes like this that sometimes push Chad away. He's not aware that Melissa has her own issues she fights internally every day and that she doesn't really mean the sarcastic and selfish words that come out of her mouth. Melissa is naturally a caring, humble, and compassionate girl who cares about others, but the negative thoughts in her head overtake her sense of reason.

Melissa has been urging Chad to get a car ever since he started working, telling him it would be a good look for them.

The idea of a car crossed his mind, but he has never tried to turn that idea into reality. With her nonstop pestering, he begins saving for a down payment. For his birthday, his dad gives him $1,000 to put in his savings account toward the purchase of a car, with an agreement that he has to save $700 of his own money first. He tells him it's their little secret and not to tell his grandfather. He doesn't want Poppa P to know, because when he originally got wind that Chad wanted a car, he gave him a long lecture. Chad recalls Poppa P speech.

"It's not a good idea to take your money and use it for a down payment for a car just yet. It's not a need. Public transportation is practically on every corner. Learn how to save your money instead of spending it down to your last penny. A car is a liability, not an asset. An asset is something that makes you money with little or no participation. It puts money in your pocket. Just because it sounds like an asset, smells like an asset, looks like an asset, or is on your behind like an asset, that doesn't mean it's an asset. Rental property, artwork, real estate, stocks, a business—these are all assets. Wasting your earnings on momentary gratification will push you further away from your life's mission, whatever that may be. And just so you know, rapping isn't it." For emphasis, he swings his hand. "Look at you. Dressed in all your designer gear. Everything you have on is a liability: that shirt, those boots, and those jeans. I bet you think it's an asset because you paid a lot of money for it. Wrong! It's a liability. Say it with me. Li-a-bil-i-ty. A liability is something that takes money out of your pocket. As soon as money touches your hand, you immediately go out and spend it on cars, clothes, and unnecessary junk, which all lose value once purchased. So instead of spending all your free time shopping, invest in yourself, your future."

But even after that long speech, he doesn't change his mind about buying a car, and Melissa's influence only amplifies the urge. Even Addison suggests he listen to his grandfather's advice. Against his better judgment, he doesn't heed the advice and starts to save for a new car. He adds more money to the account and is proud of what he has accumulated. Every time he looks at his money growing, it motivates him to keep saving.

Returning to the present and Melissa's sour mood, Chad says, "I'm working on it," too tired of her complaining to say more.

Key Points

- To put it simply, credit is about borrowing money. Credit refers to the ability of a person or a business to borrow money from a lender with the intent or promise to pay the money back.

- With loans and credit cards, people are able to borrow the money they need to buy something now.

- Earning credit requires earning people's trust. When you borrow money from a parent, guardian, neighbor, or friend, you usually promise to pay it back by a certain time. They lend you the money because they trust you to keep your promise. The same holds true when you borrow from a bank.

- Taking personal responsibility is absolutely essential when it comes to credit. Taking personal responsibility means keeping your promise to pay back the money you owe.

- Not everyone can borrow money from a bank. Credit is a privilege, and it's granted only to those who have demonstrated their ability to manage their money over time. This is called one's credit history.

Questions

1. A negative credit rating affects your life in what way?
2. What is a FICO score?
3. What number is considered a bad FICO score?
4. List things you consider to be assets. Why are they assets?
5. List things you consider to be liabilities. Why are they liabilities?

CHAPTER 8

Battle Rap

Everything is going well. Chad's been working extra hours to save more money for his car and is looking into colleges with genuine interest. The only problem is that his manager is getting on his last nerve. He's been riding Chad about the way he responds to customers, how he takes longer than the allowed break time, and anything else he can find. Chad thinks about quitting on several occasions, but each time he thinks about it, his family comes to mind. He doesn't want to disappoint them.

"Next," Chad calls out to the next customer.

"Um … um … let me get a box of Goobers … umm … M&Ms, and two small Cokes. What do you want, Tiana?" the customer asks the little girl standing next to her.

"Um … a bag of popcorn and a blue slushy."

"Will that be all?" Chad asks the customer.

"Yeah … you know what … change the Goobers for … umm … a box of Whoppers," the customer responds hesitantly.

"Is that your final answer?" Chad asks with a poker face.

"What?" The customer has a confused facial expression, and his tone reveals he's annoyed. Chad is annoyed as well. He muses, *Why can't people figure out what they want before they get up here? After standing in line for almost ten minutes, you would think they would already know what they want. Plan your order ahead of time. Don't make no sense … holding up the entire line.*

58

"I asked would that be all," Chad responds.

"Yeah. How much?" the customer asks, still giving Chad a funny look. *Oh boy, here it comes*, Chad thinks before giving the customer a total.

"Fifteen dollars and forty cents."

"What! Sixteen dollars. What the heck did I buy?" the customer exclaims.

"Fifteen dollars and forty cents, not sixteen dollars," Chad corrects.

"Fifteen dollars and forty cents, sixteen dollars—what's the difference?"

"Sixty cents," Chad states with a blank stare.

The manager is nearby at another concession, watching the exchange. He's had many conversations with Chad about his abrupt interactions with customers. Chad keeps the other employees in stitches, but the manager doesn't find the situation funny at all. The manager knows firsthand what it's like dealing with obnoxious, rude, impatient customers. However, it's still the duty of the employee to remain professional and patient. The manager walks over to Chad. "When you are finished serving that customer, please come and take a walk with me."

Oh boy.

After the manager reprimands him, Chad brushes it off and returns to work. The day is drawn out with the usual hustle of customers. During break, Chad bumps into Jay and some of his other friends. While horsing around with them, he gets into some friendly banter with one of his coworkers about who is the best rapper of all time. The bantering spills into a rap battle. A small group of workers eggs them on.

Why not? Chad thinks. *This will be good practice for the upcoming competition.*

The group bands together in the back, one on the lookout for the manager and others with cell phones in their hands, video ready, while Chad and his opponent take their stance to prepare for battle. Jay gives Chad a nod and mouths, "Do your thang."

Gaining momentum from his boy's support, Chad starts defending his rapping ability. His words are good, but not flowing smoothly as he envisioned. His lyrics don't mirror who he really is. They don't sound authentic. They seem fake and forced. Trying to build up his street cred by using gangsta lyrics isn't working. Determined not to give up, he presses on. When he's done, a few claps can be heard. His opponent takes center, and the words flow smoothly and effortlessly from his mouth, shattering Chad's world.

The other rapper's lyrics are coming straight from a real-life diary, poetically spoken by a person who has been hurt, angered, and empowered. His personal journal is rolled into this battle with a magnetic energy felt by the spectators. There isn't a hint of phoniness. When he's done, the audience is silent. They forgot they were at the theater. Chad's opponent has a hypnotizing force that pulls the crowd into his world. When Chad comes to, he is staggering, trying to regain his composure. He's deafened by the group's cheering and laughter. Chad realizes he's way out of his league. Mortified but refusing to show his true feelings, he humbly takes his beating by giving props to his opponent.

"What the heck is going on back here?"

Even though Chad was reprimanded earlier, he is relieved to hear that voice, the voice that under normal circumstances would make him cringe. However, these aren't normal circumstances, and he is actually glad to see the manager. Chad knows they are in trouble, especially him since the manager just spoke with him earlier about his impatience with customers, but he doesn't care. He's just glad the manager came over when he did, saving Chad from further embarrassment. He threatens them all, immediately zooming his attention on Chad.

"Every time I turn around, you're back here, rapping or battling it out and then returning from your break late. Time is money! There are customers that need to be serviced, and you keep leaving your coworkers to work double duty to pull your load. That's it! I'm done warning you! The next time I catch you rapping it out, you'll be fired."

Sighs can be heard. Someone in the crowd says, "Really, dude? Who made you the hip-hop cop?"

The manager whips his head around. "Who said that?" His question is met with laughter. "Okay, we'll see who gets the last laugh."

Before storming off, he turns his attention back to Chad, "The ice you're standing on is very thin." He pauses and points to the floor. "Oh look, there's a crack. And you're about to fall through. I'm watching you."

Once the laughing dies down, the group returns to work but not before Jay pulls Chad to the side.

Giving him a pound, he says, "Your manager is bugged." They both laugh. "But on a serious note, you're a good dude. But that rap competition that's coming up is no joke. A word of advice. You gonna have to come with it. I know it's hard when you're the first to spit because it gives the opponent an advantage to make comebacks, but vocally you're not connecting with your lyrics. You have to live the words. Put some more buzz into your performance. Let it resonate like your life depends on it."

Chad muses, *I'm tired of people telling me what to do!* Humiliation clouding his judgment, Chad allows his bruised ego to speak. "White boy trying to school *me* on rap! What? You think you Eminem now?" *This is my brother. I didn't mean that.*

Taken aback and offended by the remark, Jay retorts, "Nah. This white boy isn't Eminem, nor do I wanna be him. You see, I'm repping me. The real me."

"What you tryin' to say?"

Squaring up, Jay takes a step closer with a deadly stare. "I'm not *tryin'* to say somethin'. I said it. You're on some bogus bull—"

"Either row or get off the ship!" the manager shouts while walking up to the two best-friends-turned-enemies. "You still got your butt anchored like you don't have customers to serve." Chad backs down.

Jay, not threatened by the manager's presence, slips in, "This white boy *earned* the cred to offer you advice. I got the full trophy case and a savings account with all the money I won to prove it. What do you got? Oh, my bad, no trophy case for your invisible trophies, and do you *even have* a savings account?" Jay walks off, not giving Chad a chance to respond.

Chad feels instantly remorseful. Jay is one of his best friends, who wants only the best for him. Chad is surprised by his own words. *I know he meant well.* Though he knows he should go after Jay to apologize, he doesn't. Instead he stands rooted in place, allowing his ego to dictate his actions.

For the remainder of the evening, Chad relives his embarrassing loss and his out-of-line comments to Jay. Over and over again, the battle replays in his head. This isn't the first battle rap he lost in the theater. He had a few battles with two other rappers, who were blazingly skilled, and he lost each time. This battle was the worst. His pursuit of rapping is causing him grief on and off the job. Sneaking off to the side to practice lyrics and having small rapping competitions with other rappers is always causing him to come back late from his breaks. *Being fired could be a good thing. Then I will be able to devote more time to practicing without any interruptions,* he thinks. He decides to talk the matter over with Melissa before he makes a final decision.

Later that evening, while preparing to clock out, Chad's phone vibrates. It's a text from Melissa.

"Hey boo, r u off yet?"

"Just clocked out. WYD?"

"Watching TV. How was work?"

"It was okay. Had a battle. Lost."

"Don't worry. I bet u were better anyway. What do they know?"

"I might not enter the competition."

"WHAT?! R U CRAZY!! And miss our chance of hitting it big time? U can't quit. Baby, ur good. U just have to practice more. Hip-hop is what u love."

"Is it?"

"Of course it is. Look how long you've been talking about all the money u can make when u get a record deal. I can c us now. Our own reality show! I'm still writing down ideas to pitch. A rich and famous high school couple in love. U winning the competition and getting a chance to perform on the Hip-Hop award show will make a great story line. Red carpet and all! They ain't ready 4 us." Clearly, Melissa desperately wants to live the hip-hop fairy tale. "Hey maybe you can buy a book. Rapping for dummies."

"They got that?!"

"idk wouldn't hurt to search."

"So I guess ur saying that I can't rap."

"I'm not saying that. I'm just trying to help."

"yr not."

"4get u then."

"4gotten."

"Ouch! Help yrself. BYE!"

She's no help, Chad thinks while riding the bus home. He's mad at the world. *Stupid manager. If he wasn't hassling me so much, I would be able to concentrate on my lyrics for the competition. And simple Mel, calling me a dummy rapper. Maybe she needs to buy* How to Be Smart for Dummies.

"I just need to quit," he mumbles to himself.

CHAPTER 9

Authenticity

Chad doesn't quit. But to mask his feelings and comfort his bruised ego, he starts spending money frivolously, buying whatever he desires at the moment. To make matters worse, Jay isn't speaking to him, and his relationship with Melissa is deteriorating. Everything seems to set the couple off, especially the rap competition. And if Chad inadvertently mentions any advice given by Addison, Melissa's infuriation magnifies ten times over. The arguments and their discomfort with each other drive Chad to confide in Addison even more. Addison is the only one in the world with whom he feels he can be himself. He feels understood and doesn't have to worry about being judged.

Time goes on, and he is still harboring feelings about his lost rap battle at work. Whenever his mind takes a vacation from the memory, somebody at his job is waiting in the shadows to recap the embarrassing scene. To make matters worse, somebody videotaped the battle and posted it on social media. Some of the comments were brutal.

To escape his bruised mental state, he redirects his frustration to his personal finances. Every pay week, he spends his entire check down to the lint in his pockets. Saving is a thing of the past. The money he's accumulated depletes entirely, including the money his father contributed for a car. This fact weighs heavily on his mind. To compound the situation, he reneges on his contract agreement with his mother to pay his outstanding balance in full and on time each month. There are times when he doesn't pay the balance at all. The balance is almost reaching the card's fifteen hundred limit.

He finds solace in writing poetry and spending money. It's the only thing that gives him pleasure and keeps him sane. His time is spent hopping from store to store, compulsively spending money with Melissa in tow, buying anything that will temporarily remedy his battered feelings and boost Melissa's negative self-image. Their pursuit of the ideal image combined with instant gratification creates the illusion of being in control and offers freedom from negative self-esteem issues. The job he once appreciated becomes a thing of the past. Chad fails to realize that life comes with many challenges, and it's the way he deals with the challenges that will determine his fate. He has yet to learn that he should never let anyone, or anything deter him.

———

Chad is on break, composing poetry on a piece of paper. He sits at a back table in tune with the words and ideas that come with ease. Addison comes and breaks his concentration.

"Hey, before you went on break, you were telling me about the rap battle you lost the other day."

"Yeah, I got roasted," Chad says disgustedly. "I don't think I'm good enough for the rap competition. The hours I work aren't leaving me enough time to practice. The manager is always lurking somewhere. I should just take Melissa's advice and quit. I'm seriously thinking about it."

"Either you going to take her advice or mine. Be decisive and make up your mind." Addison continues, "Maybe your heart isn't really into rapping. Be honest with yourself and ask why you're doing it and who you are doing it for."

"Yeah, I know. You're right. I really do need to start being true to myself. I'm done. I'm quitting this stupid job. Really don't need it anyway being that I'm still under my parents' care."

"Who do you think you're fooling? You don't want to depend on your parents like that. It's only those who are persistent and willing to stay the course, despite the obstacles, that achieve their goals."

"Yeah, yeah, yeah, later for all that," Chad retorts. "Like I said, my manager is getting on my last nerve anyway."

"I'm quite sure you have nerves to spare," Addison says. "Besides, I wasn't talking about your job. I meant being true to yourself regarding rapping. Being a rapper isn't the only way to express yourself."

"What? What are you talking about?" Sometimes Chad doesn't know who he hates talking to more, Addison or Melissa. At this point, he finds them both annoying.

Addison continues, "Let's think for a moment. Why *did* you accept that challenge?" As Chad ponders the question, Addison's innocence and honesty strike a chord, ridding him of his anger.

"I had no other choice. I had to go along with it," he humbly answers, despising himself for being a fraud.

"After he challenged you, what did you do next?" Addison asks.

"I tried to intimidate him. I spit out words about murder, gangs, and some other stuff. Then I ended my line with 'Do you know who I am?'"

"Did he? Did the opponent really believe that?" Addison asks.

"I guess. I went hard so he would believe the lyrics I was spitting."

"Do you believe it? Do you know who you are?" Addison's questions baffle him. He wonders how to answer honestly. He feels tortured, caught in between two different worlds. A boy in the middle. A weird feeling creeps over him. Addison seems so sure of things, authentic, not swayed by the opinions of others.

"I have to finish what I started," he solemnly responds, without much conviction. Addison is filled with compassion, feeling his pain.

He thinks about the rappers he admires, whose images and past experiences have awed him so many times, the real hip-hop legends who fought to be where they are now and love what they do. They have lived their words, lived through the hardships of life. At one point or another, they probably felt trapped in their harsh realities. Some didn't even have the same advantages he did, and here he is, lying to himself and anybody who will listen about living and understanding their experiences. The rappers he admires stand on the edge, not in the middle. They have taken their stand and lived with the consequences.

"I hate it. I'm starting to really hate my job."

"Your job?" Addison asks, not believing it's his job that Chad hates but something more, hoping Chad will finally admit the truth and stop the self-inflicted torment.

"Yeah. I'm sick of the long line of customers, waiting to buy a funnel cake. Who stands in a line for thirty minutes, waiting for a funnel cake anyway?" Chad retorts.

"You need to ask that the next time you stand on a one-day, two-block-long, around-the-corner, over-the-bridge line, waiting for a store to open just to cop a pair of sneakers," Addison says.

"And your point is? You can't compare a funnel cake to a pair of dope sneakers."

"I just did."

"I'm starting to hate my manager too," Chad complains.

"Your manager? Why?" Addison asks.

"Because if it wasn't for him stressing me out, I could probably put better lyrics together."

"But the lyrics will still be false," Addison challenges.

"Then I hate hip-hop!"

"Hip-hop?" Addison probes.

"Myself," he snaps.

"Yourself?" Addison probes further.

Exasperated and understanding Addison's insinuation, he finally admits, "The person I *claim* to be. I hate the person I *claim* to be." Chad feels an immediate sense of relief.

"What will you do?" Addison asks.

Chad has no answer. He becomes defensive. "A lot of rappers fake it. If it's not me, there will be other rappers doing the same thing."

Addison isn't buying it, and Chad isn't buying it either. Taking a slow, deep breath, he asks Addison, "What do you believe? What do you really believe?"

"I believe you are afraid that if you embrace your true self and introduce it to the world, you will not be accepted. So instead you hide behind a facade and go along with whatever society deems acceptable. You love hip-hop and admire many rappers, but you don't want to become one. You like writing poetry, and you're good at it, but since you don't think society has deemed poetry 'cool,' you refuse to embrace your true self and just go along with what others think. That is what makes you unhappy and confused."

Chad realizes that Addison has forced him to understand the essential truth. His unhappiness and discontent with himself can't be blamed on his job, hip-hop, or anyone else; it's all up to him. He remembers Poppa P's words: "A man should always be accountable for his actions."

Chad says, "Melissa likes me being a rapper; she says I'm good."

"And you believe her?"

Wanting to defend Melissa, he says, "Yes. She's been right about a lot of things."

"That was then, this is now. Things and people change. Anyway, what difference does it make? You're not happy with yourself. What can Melissa or anyone else do to change that?" Addison is always reminding him of this. Chad admits that the pursuit of fame and money isn't worth selling his soul. If he continues like this, there is a possibility of losing himself and never amounting to what he is really destined to be. He doesn't like feeling trapped.

"What if you didn't enter the competition?" Addison asks.

"You mean, just stop practicing for it and everything?"

"Yeah," Addison says, "and tell Melissa and Jay the truth: that you don't want to do it. But not before you apologize to Jay first. And don't leave room for Melissa or anybody else to change your mind. Stand firm in your decision."

It makes sense to him, and he wonders why he didn't relieve himself of all the anguish a while ago.

Addison adds, "Melissa is living an illusion. And your life is a lie. Take a look at your book of rap lyrics. From what I've seen, you write about a world you never experienced. Those lyrics aren't you."

Deep in thought, Chad stares at the ground. *I'm writing about things people find acceptable and are eager to hear, and my willingness to sell my true identity always leaves me feeling depressed. I used to be proud of things I wrote about. I have to admit ... I am a phony. When I accept me for me, I will be able to concentrate on other things, like writing poetry, applying for college, and choosing a major I'm actually interested in.*

"Yeah, you're right. I'm done with the lying. Either people can accept me for who I am or kick rocks."

Addison beams, relieved that Chad is finally coming around. "I will accept you no matter what you decide."

He feels at peace. He's not sure why he feels so comforted by this revelation. Maybe it's because he liked the way Addison gave him a deep sense of connection, drawing him to the person he was created to be and not this false image he was creating for himself.

CHAPTER 10

The Nipsey Hussle

Chad finally takes Addison's advice and apologizes to Jay for the distasteful comments he made on the day he lost the battle. He goes on to thank Jay for always having his back and explains that it was his bruised ego talking. He also reminds Jay that he admires his rapping skills. Jay accepts the apology, knowing Chad was speaking from misguided anger. They've known each other too long to let a few bad words come between them.

While Chad might have taken Addison's advice on mending his friendship with Jay right away, it remains a continual push to adjust his financial attitude. Addison presses Chad about the way he's been disrespecting his parents' financial trust. Internally, he knows he's wrong. He's afraid, more than he's willing to admit, of scarring his relationship with them. Determined to regain his integrity, Chad starts saving money again to repay his dad, but the amount is far less than what he was originally saving each week. He is still spending much more than he is saving. Each pay week, he leaves a small amount in his savings account for his debt, and the rest he spends on whatever he or Melissa wants.

Melissa's jealousy intensifies her adverse behavior. The more Chad mentions good advice given by Addison, the more Melissa spews the opposite. If Chad mentions Addison's suggestion that he should save, Melissa influences him to spend. Her fallback line is, "We have to look the part." If he mentions Addison's idea to put more effort into college than rapping, Melissa says he should put more effort into rapping. In Melissa's mind, this is how she maintains control. Little does she know that trying to have that control is doing more damage to their relationship. She makes several attempts to meet Addison, but every time she goes to Chad's job, he says Addison isn't working that shift, even on the occasions when Melissa arrives unannounced.

"This dude is getting on my last nerve. He's pushing me one step closer to quitting," Chad complains to Melissa about his manager over the telephone. "Just the other day he complained about me being a minute late from my break, a minute late. Really? So I asked him what he was doing just standing around, waiting for me, counting the seconds." His gripe is met with silence. "Hello. Are you there?" Chad asks.

"Yeah, yeah, yeah," Melissa responds half-heartedly. Today is one of the many days she sits in front of the TV, watching programs that feed her insecurities. Like most days, they leave her in a funk.

"Her boobs are fake!" Melissa says.

"What? Am I interrupting your date with another reality show?" Chad asks impatiently. Frustrated, he continues dumping his negative load on Melissa. "Why do you always say that? How would you know whether they are fake or not? Not everybody is born with small breasts."

Not wanting to get in a debate, she snickers guiltily. "Okay, I'm sorry." Turning her attention away from the TV, she gives Chad her complete focus. "If you feel that way about your job, quit. That job has been taking your time away from practicing rap anyway." Melissa secretly wants him to quit because of her pent-up jealousy toward Addison. She hates their relationship and the fact that Chad seems to value another's opinion besides hers.

"The only thing that keeps me working there is that I want to pay my dad back the money he gave me for the car."

"But he *gave* you the money," Melissa says.

"Yeah, I know, but when he gave it to me, it was to support my dream of getting a car. I still feel obligated to pay him back since I stopped saving for the goal he supported."

"What are you doing about the car situation?"

"Not much since I spent all the money I was saving for it."

"What? Why? When?"

"When me and you were hanging out, having fun, and running to the mall—that's when," Chad answers, irate.

"You sound like you're blaming me," Melissa responds.

"I'm not blaming you. I'm just saying."

"What are you saying, Chad?"

"I'm saying that you are always suggesting I buy this or that to dress the part of a famous rapper. If you haven't noticed, I'm not famous, and every time I buy something, like a pair of sneakers for myself, you say, "Oh, I want a pair too. It would be cute if we were matching.' Well, it's not so cute when our pockets are matching zero, is it?"

"So you *are* blaming me," Melissa whines.

"I blame myself, but you were no help. You weren't satisfied with just getting an original pair of sneakers. You have to be all extra and get yours engraved with all the bells and whistles and stuff. Like putting spinning rims on an already-fancy car."

Melissa says angrily, "You say I was no help, but I bet Addison is a big help, right?"

"Addison has nothing to do with it."

"Addison has plenty to do with it. All I hear is, Addison said this, Addison said that, like she knows what's best for you or something."

Before he knows it, Chad says, "Maybe Addison does."

"Oh, yeah? Well, does she know this?" *Click.*

"Hello. Hello?" *Did she just hang up on me? Okay, I know someone who won't mind hearing me out and helping me figure out my problems.*

Weeks go by, and Chad is still putting money aside to repay his dad for the car. He can't believe that all the money he saved and was proud of is now gone, all because of his pursuit of something that was probably not meant to be. The debt he accumulated while chasing a false sense of identity, depleting his entire savings, plus the loss of the money his father contributed for a car, burdens his psyche with guilt. Chad's father discovered the money was spent when he stumbled on a bank statement haphazardly left out in the open. Disappointed in himself for letting his father down, Chad flops on the bed, admitting this to Addison, who accompanied him home after they got off from work. He recalls the entire scenario.

"Chad ... Chad."

Chad wakes up with a frightened but relieved expression on his face, glad to see his dad standing in front of him. He was in the middle of a nightmare, where those same villains from his previous nightmares were chasing him. Ignoring his son's expression, Vincent holds out Chad's bank statement and asks, "What is this?"

"What is what?" Chad answers stupidly.

"Boy, don't play with me. You see what I'm holding. It's your bank statement! You had it laid out on your dresser. I took a look, expecting to see at least five hundred dollars added to the money I gave you, but from what I can see, you only have twenty-five dollars in your account. What happened to the one thousand dollars I gave you and the money you were supposed to add to it?"

Looking at his dad's face, Chad thinks he would've been better off left in his nightmare with the villains.

Chad slowly sits up in bed, making sure not to get too close to his dad. Vincent waves the bank statement around like he is about to slap him with it. Chad stutters for a moment and finally gets something out that's audible.

"I can explain."

Vincent quietly stares at Chad.

"I said, I can explain," Chad repeats.

"I heard you the first time."

Chad stammers, "Um … Um … What had happened was …"

"What happened was, you didn't take my advice," Poppa P interjects, walking into the bedroom. "I talked to you before about instant gratification. You should be able to save at least a dime out of every dollar. You let material things control your good senses. Weren't you listening when I gave you that speech a while back? No, you were probably busy sonogramming and all that other stuff you young folks do."

"It's Instagramming."

"Instagram, Sonogram, Moneygram—who cares?" He stares at Chad for a moment and continues, "I thought you were listening, Son. What happened? You were doing so good." He directs his stare at Vincent. "You thought I didn't know about the money you gave him to put toward a new car," he says. Vincent is about to comment, but Poppa P quickly dismisses him with the wave of his hand.

Chad explains how his manager has been getting on his nerves and makes a bunch of other excuses.

When he's done, Poppa P says, "Excuses, excuses, excuses. A man doesn't make excuses. He owns up to what he's done. And you're not doing that. Instead, you're blaming another man for your problems and your actions. Let me tell you something, Son. In life you are going to come across many obstacles. There is no way around them. However, it's not the obstacles that make you who you are, but it's how you handle those obstacles that determines your character. So, you say the manager is riding you over nonsense. Maybe that's true, but his attitude should not deter you from your plans. If your plans were to save money, nothing should have taken you off that course. You have to believe that you're stronger than that. If anything, it should make you more determined and creative. Think of ways to improve yourself and find a more productive solution."

Vincent tries to get back in the conversation, but Poppa P quickly shushes him. "I'm the oldest in this room—the father! And the grandfather! Now, since you are so determined to be a rapper, why don't you do the Nipsey Hussle?"

"Huh? You don't know nothin' about Nipsey," Chad says.

"I know enough to understand the impact he made as a community activist and his role as an entrepreneur, taking his earned money and opening a clothing store in his community and offering jobs to people that looked like him. And if you were business minded like him, you would heed the words of his record label: All Money In, No Money Out." Poppa P winks before continuing. "You think this old man doesn't know a thing about you young folks." He stares at the dumbfounded expression on Chad's face.

After hearing the story, Addison remains silent, giving him that deep, soul-searching pause that sometimes makes Chad uncomfortable. Knowing already what's about to come, he flops his head down onto the pillow and prepares himself.

"Every time I try to give you advice, you turn a deaf ear and come back with more complaints," Addison argues.

Not wanting to hear it, Chad snaps, "First it's Melissa with her attitude, and now it's you!"

"Since you don't want to hear me out, I'll just leave.

After Addison's departure, Chad falls into a fitful sleep. His nightmare returns soon as his lids touch.

Ms. Mystery Fee is back, lurking, awaiting his return. For a while she rides him like a donkey while yelling, "Collection! Agency! Sic 'em!"

From a distance, he sees two drooling, vicious-looking rottweilers. "*Boo woof, boo woof.*" Their barks echo through the air as they charge his way at full speed.

Chad swings Ms. Mystery Fee to the ground and takes off running. From behind, he hears their vicious barks mixed with Ms. Mystery Fee's commands. "Sic 'em!"

"*Boo woof, boo woof.*" The sounds of their barks are getting nearer.

Chad opens his mouth to scream as he falls forward from the impact of the dogs knocking him to the ground. Chad rolls over swinging his arms while he calls for help.

Relief comes when he sees a gray-suited silhouette, a mirror image of himself, standing at a close distance. Chad reaches out and cries for help, but the image stands there, staring at him. With a look of despair, Chad calls out to the image again, begging for help. After a moment, the image glides over but doesn't grasp Chad's outstretched hand. It ignores Chad's plea before faintly disappearing. The dogs are growling and biting into him. Chad wrestles with all his might to break free.

"Boy, what is wrong with you?" Poppa P asks, standing over him. Chad's eyes spring open, blurry with tears.

"Are you okay, Son? What got you crying in your sleep?"

A bit embarrassed, Chad brushes it off with, "A lot is going on."

"What? You finally dreamed you're not a rapper?" Poppa P asks humorously. "Come on. Get up and wash your face. Let's take a ride in my car to get something to eat. Some air would do you good."

Chad makes an all-out effort, trying to dig a way out of his self-made hole. His manager remains relentless and continues to ride him every chance he gets. But Chad remains humble, grits his teeth, and requests longer hours. He wants to quickly repay his dad and pay off his credit card bills.

While at work, Chad sits eating and looking over his credit card statement—dreading the day his mother finds out he maxed out his credit card. He doesn't know what's gotten into him. *It seems like the more I try, the more things get in the way*, he thinks.

Chad is tormented with guilt. His parents trusted him. He let his dad down, and now he is letting his mom down by burying himself deeper in debt. He owes them both. He's trying to figure a way out of the mess he made and a way to repay them, especially now that his manager is threatening to fire him.

"If I'm fired, I won't be able to pay them back," he says aloud. He let his selfishness and material obsession damage his trust with those who love him, including himself. All of the things that once brought him joy are now making him distressed. Feeling melancholy, he recalls Momma P's words of wisdom: *"Real joy can't be bought with superficial things, because it has no real value."*

As Chad simmers in his thoughts, Addison glides over. Glad for the intrusion and knowing he will feel better afterward, he regurgitates his dilemma and completes it with a detailed description of his unpleasant dream. After listening, Addison lets the information settle for a moment before gently saying, "Maybe your nightmares are showing you your future if you continue repeating the same old, destructive behavior. Think about it. You have a nightmare each time you lie, get lazy, goof off from work and school, or spend your money frivolously. I know this may sound a little crazy, but when you improved your actions and behavior, the nightmares stopped."

"It does sound crazy. Why would my nightmares reveal my future?"

Addison contemplates his question and twirls it around in silence before saying, "Life is complex. Dreams and one's future can be revealed in various ways. Everyone learns lessons differently. It's never the same for everyone." Chad has to admit that before, a bad dream was nothing more than a bad dream, but now these nightmares are at a whole other level. They disrupt everything: his peaceful sleep, school, and his attitude. He never had to think about a bad dream or dissect its meaning before.

Addison doesn't give up trying to help Chad make sense of his situation, offering various resolutions, and trying to convince him that there is a way out if he really wants it and tries hard enough—warning him again to come clean and be honest with his mother about his credit card and the accumulating balance and fees. Chad tells Addison he would rather wrestle with the villains in his nightmares than deal with the repercussions of telling his mother the truth.

At least in my nightmares I finally wake up, but my mom might put my lights out for good. She'll take those credit card fees and beat me to death with them, he muses.

Deciding to leave the situation alone for a moment, Addison kindly says, "It's your choice, and whatever you decide, I'm here for you, but I still think you should tell your mother" before leaving him to work it out.

He stares at his credit card statement. *Wow, look at these fees. Momma P says there's a solution to every problem, but where is the solution for this?* he wonders.

Even after the heart-to-heart with Addison, Chad decides not to tell his mom. He continues to work extra hours when possible to earn more money to pay his credit card bills without his mom being the wiser. Quitting is no longer a thought. He desperately tries to impress the manager and prove that he can change. He even becomes a little more patient with customers.

With Addison's help, he puts a plan together. He wants to repay his dad the $1,000. Each paycheck, he takes a small portion and deposits it into his savings account. He stops making purchases altogether and stops using the credit card entirely. He pays the minimum payment every month, but the balance still increases instead of decreasing. This trend has him totally confused and frustrated. He discusses the issue with Addison, who tells him to let his mother know that something is wrong with the card. Utterly afraid, he doesn't take the advice. *Maybe the credit card company is making a mistake*, he thinks. But the following month, he notices the bill has increased again without him making any new charges. This time he decides to talk to Melissa about it.

"I'm just not understanding this."

"Wait!" she exclaims, like she just discovered something. Chad, excited that Melissa may have found a solution to his problem, looks up eagerly and waits for her answer. "Maybe somebody is taking your money before it gets to the bank."

"What? That doesn't make any sense," Chad says.

"Why doesn't it? You're the one who said you pay the bill every month without making any new charges, and the balance keeps increasing. So where else could it be going?"

"When I look at my statement every month, I see where they posted the payment I made, so the money is getting to them. I just don't understand why the balance is still going up."

"You should just quit, because working at the theater doesn't seem to be getting you anywhere. All the hours you are putting in, and you still can't keep up with your bills. Plus, you already said the manager is stupid. Just listen to me for a sec. If you quit, that means you will have more time to work on your lyrics for the competition. And the money you win will be more than enough to pay your entire credit card balance and pay your dad back, *and* you will have a little left over to put back in your savings account."

Chad thinks for a moment. "Yeah, you're right about that. The money would be more than enough." Then he remembers his humiliating loss when his coworker blew him out of the water and quickly reconsiders joining the hip-hop world. "But what if I don't win? I will be without the money *and* a job."

"You have to think positive," Melissa says.

"I'm trying to think positive, but I'm also trying to be realistic," he snaps.

"Well I don't know then. ¿Por qué no le preguntas a Addison? Le preguntas todo lo demás."

"What ... what did you say?"

"Since you seem to be getting an attitude with me, I said, 'Why don't you ask Addison?' You ask her everything else. And while you're at it, ask her to teach you Spanish since you think she's so smart," Melissa says, upset that she couldn't help him solve the mystery.

Glad that he caught himself before he slipped back into his old ways, Chad is determined to keep focus and get back on track while keeping Melissa at arm's length and gravitating more toward Addison. He can't tolerate Melissa's nagging. If it's not about the competition, then it's about a car or her jealousy of Addison. The negativity is driving him insane, so he thinks it's best if he stays away for a while.

Every time she calls, he says he's at work or busy with homework. But it doesn't stop her from constantly calling him. The neglect only infuriates Melissa and makes her even more jealous.

Did You Know?

- Banks *pay you* interest on money you deposit with them. Why? Because they want to use your money to make loans to other people.

- There are two kinds of interest, simple and compound interest. Simple interest is calculated on the amount of money you deposit. Compound interest is more powerful. This interest is calculated on your deposits plus any interest you've already earned. Hence, the interest the bank paid you last month now becomes part of your new total, and you earn interest on that money too.

- Imagine if your parents gave you $100 for your birthday every year for ten years. If you put it in a savings account, you would have $1,100 or even more. That's an extra $100, and you didn't have to lift a finger.

Nipsey Hussle

1. Why do you think Nipsey Hussle named his record label "All Money In, No Money Out"?
2. What was the name of Nipsey Hussle's clothing store?
3. Why do you think Nipsey opened a clothing store in his community?

CHAPTER 11

Community Service

Since Chad won't answer Melissa's calls, she starts showing up at his job every chance she gets, trying to catch Chad with Addison. She has a gut feeling that Chad is cheating on her. She becomes determined to confront Addison with a warning to stay away from her boyfriend.

Chad remembers a promise he made to himself a while back and wants to make good on it, so he makes an appointment with the college adviser to go over his financial-aid package. As he sits in the office, waiting for his adviser, he uses the computer to do a little research on his own. While at the computer, his pocket vibrates. He pulls out his phone. As he's reading the text, he feels a tap on his shoulder. He turns around, expecting to see the adviser. It's Melissa instead.

"What are you doing here?" Chad asks her.

"You ask me that a lot lately."

"Okay, is there a problem?" Chad senses an attitude.

"Actually, I do have a problem. Who were you texting?"

"Nobody."

"Liar," says Melissa. "I just saw you with your phone."

"Okay, and what about it? It's *my* phone."

"So who were you texting."

"I said nobody, and what's with the questions?"

"I wouldn't have to question you if you weren't acting so shady lately."

"Listen, Mel, I'm not acting shady. It's just that I've been busy lately."

"Why is it that every time I call, you're busy or can't talk to me for whatever reason? I'm starting to think you got something going on with that girl, Addison. Is that why you always claiming to be busy, Chad?" Melissa invades his personal space. Raising her voice an octave, she continues, "I want to meet this Addison girl."

"I don't have to introduce you to nobody!" Chad answers back. His volume now matching hers.

"Is there a problem in here?" an authoritative voice interrupts.

They both turn their attention to the guidance counselor as he walks through the door. They straighten up. He's not one to be played with. When he first started working at the school, students tried running over him because of his youthful appearance—on many occasions being mistaken for a student—but he put that in check immediately and let it be known what he did and didn't tolerate. He is handsome, tall, and well dressed, and has a no-nonsense air about him.

Female students love visiting his office and make every academic excuse to make an appointment with him. A few female teachers are no different; they also vie for his attention.

He's young, with only two years of experience. He genuinely cares about his students. His passion for helping others comes from his upbringing. Raised by his grandmother, who lacked the understanding of the intricacies involved in the modern teenager and high school life, he was left to navigate the process on his own and now seeks to help others through their tumultuous years. During his years attending high school the staff didn't really care about the students. Their focus was on getting their paychecks and watching the big, round, dusty clock hanging in back of the classroom. A volunteer from the Boys & Girls Clubs of America took him under her wing and helped with the college process, ensuring all financial assistance possible was made available to him.

"I asked if there was a problem in here."

"No ... no problem," Melissa says, backing away from Chad. "I have to get to class. We'll finish this later." She brushes past the college adviser on the way out.

"Is everything okay?" the adviser asks.

"Yeah, I'm good."

"How are your classes going?"

"They're okay. I was having a little trouble in my science class, but the teacher gave me extra help on the side. She's a cool teacher. She makes the subject interesting. I like the class."

"That's good. We need more teachers like her, but we also need more students like you, who care about their studies and visit the guidance counselor to keep track of their classes. Habits like yours take a lot of the burden off the teachers. Teachers like her make the student's life less difficult. It goes hand in hand."

"Yeah ... that sounds like a fair exchange, I guess," Chad responds.

"Is there any subject you find most interesting? A subject you would like to pursue as a major in college?" The counselor asks.

"I like math, so I was thinking about accounting ... maybe."

"Why maybe?" the counselor probes.

Chad is still unsure whether he wants to attend college even though he's taking all the necessary steps to get in one. He lies, "Because I'm still weighing my options."

The counselor responds by nodding. He averts his attention back to the computer screen. "Do you have a list of colleges you're interested in?"

"Yeah, two state schools and one private. But I'm leaning more toward state schools. They seem more affordable." He remembers that information from last year.

"Yes, I agree. One thing about taking out student loans is that they will come after you until you pay the debt entirely. But we will get to the loan portion in a minute. I want to talk to you about the SAT. You took it a second time at the beginning of the school year, and your score improved. Have you sent the new scores to the colleges of your choice yet?"

"No, not yet."

"Okay. Send them in as soon as you can. The deadline is December or January. I want you to start preparing your college applications and pay close attention to deadlines," the counselor emphasizes.

"Got it," Chad says.

"I will have your transcript and a letter of recommendation prepared before the deadline. In the meantime, please ask a few teachers to do the same."

Chad's phone vibrates again. While the counselor is looking at the computer, Chad sneaks a peek at the screen. It's a text from Melissa: "R U STILL N GC OFFICE?!!"

"Did you do any research about the cost of college and financial aid like I asked?" The counselor is talking while looking at the computer screen. Chad is about to answer, but the vibration of his phone interrupts his thoughts. He takes another quick look to see who texted him, and it's Melissa again. He immediately turns his attention back to the guidance counselor without reading it.

"Yeah I did. I found out that there are three types of financial aid: grants, work studies, and loans." The counselor stares at him. Chad stares back.

After a moment, the counselor says, "Okay, so could you give me a brief overview of each category?"

This dude really wants me to explain financial aid? Letting off a sigh, Chad answers, "There are four different kinds of grants: Federal Pell Grants, Federal Supplemental Educational Opportunity Grants, Iraq and Afghanistan Service Grants ... I can't remember the other one."

"It's the Teacher Education Assistance Grant," the counselor reminds him. "What are the other types of financial aid?"

"There is the Federal Work Study where a grant is given to the college student who work on or off campus and is paid federal minimum wage, and the other is the Stafford Loan Program, the Direct Subsidized Loan, Direct Unsubsidized Loan, and Direct Parent PLUS Loan."

The counselor confirms with a nod of his head.

"Let me ask you a question."

"Shoot."

"How do I apply for a Stafford Loan?" Chad asks.

"By filling out a FAFSA application. Do you know what FAFSA stands for?"

"No."

"It stands for Free Application for Federal Student Aid. Every year, FAFSA forms are available on January first. Fafsa.edu.gov is the website to fill out the form. It's best to do it as early as possible. Each college has its own deadline, so make sure you know their dates. I advise you to do this as soon as possible just in case any corrections are needed." The counselor takes a breath and continues, "A FAFSA must be completed to determine a family's eligibility for financial aid. Depending on the scholarships and grants received, the student will have to make up the difference by taking out loans."

Chad interrupts, "What is the difference between subsidized and unsubsidized?"

"The subsidized loan is available to undergraduate students based on financial need. What's good about this program is that the government pays the interest on the loan while you're in school and during a six-month grace period after graduating or leaving school, and the unsubsidized loan is available to undergraduate and graduate students regardless of financial need. The student is responsible for paying the interest while in school, or it will continue to accumulate while the student is still in school. Here look this up." He takes a sticky and writes down the website for more information: studentaid.gov/understand-aid/types/loans.

"This is the website for more information regarding Stafford Loans. Plus, it has calculators to help estimate your payments based on different plan options. It's a good site."

"What is the maximum I can borrow?"

"Each academic class has a maximum Stafford Loan limit."

Academic	Maximum Stafford Loan Limit
Freshman	$5,500 (no more than $3,500 may be subsidized by the federal government)
Sophomore	$6,500 (no more than $4,500 may be subsidized by the federal government)
Junior and Senior	$7,500 (no more than $5,500 may be subsidized by the federal government)

They continue.

"If the financial aid package and Stafford Loans aren't sufficient, then your parents can apply for the PLUS Loan." Chad did a little research beforehand and found a lot of information on Parent PLUS Loans, which he feels he would be able to articulate in a clear manner.

"I did some research on Parent PLUS Loans."

"Okay, good. And what did you come up with? What are the benefits of a Parent PLUS Loan?" the counselor asks proudly. He is really impressed that Chad did his own research. Chad knows the counselor is testing him, but it's all good. He's prepared.

He indulges his adviser. "For one, with a PLUS Loan the parent doesn't have to start making payments until after the student graduates."

The counselor smiles and interrupts, "In which case, knowing that you are *such* a good son, you will be getting a job to help your parents repay the loan."

Chad agrees with a smirk before continuing. "Another benefit is that the Parent PLUS Loan is forgiven if the parent becomes disabled or dies."

"That's good, Chad. It seems you've been doing your research, and I must say, you're very good at articulating the information." He pauses. "Listen. You remember I told you that the community center is looking for volunteers to help students navigate the college process. Did you sign up?"

Timidly, Chad says "no."

"You really need to think about it. The greatest success you will ever experience will be helping others to succeed and grow. I volunteer at the Boys & Girls Club, and I tell you, the feeling I get from helping others is exhilarating. To know I'm making a difference in someone else's life is a joy beyond measure. Once you experience that feeling, it's addictive. You start looking for other ways to positively impact lives. There's no greater feeling than knowing you made a difference in someone else's life."

Can I make a difference as a rapper? Chad thinks.

"You should try it. I guarantee you will feel totally awesome. If you don't, you can come back and tell me I was wrong." His counselor smiles. "That'll be part of the legacy you leave behind, that you helped others obtain success. That's a nice way to be remembered. Everyone, including you, stands to gain. The giving of your time will empower others and boost your spirit. By serving others, you're also helping yourself. The giving of your time would be a great service to the community, and it will look good on your college application. That's one of the main things they look for."

The guidance counselor shuffles some papers around on his desk, retrieving a stack of documents. "This is a list of organizations where you can volunteer your services: food banks, homeless shelters, Ronald McDonald House, Special Olympics, helping others learn to read, libraries, senior citizen centers, animal shelters. And you can network with other young people who are working for a cause. You can also pick up litter in your neighborhood."

Picking up trash ... Is this dude for real? I don't even keep my own room clean. I can just hear Poppa P now if he finds out I'm keeping the streets clean and not the house.

"Chad ... Chad!" The guidance counselor interrupts his thoughts. "Would you be interested in volunteering?"

"Oh ...um ... I don't know." Chad mulls over the request he put in at work for extra work hours to help pay off his debt sooner. "I have a lot going on right now. Most of my free time is spent working."

"Oh, I see. Well, think about it. Good grades and high test scores can definitely help when applying for college, but college admissions staff also take into account other things like your interests, hobbies, and school and community-based extracurricular activities on applications." He looks Chad in the eye. "And Chad, concerning your long hours at work ... sometimes it's not *always* about working harder; it's about working smarter."

Whatever that means. Chad nods, not too convinced. As if reading Chad's mind, the guidance counselor says, "Working hard is good only to a certain point. You have to learn how to work smarter. First, you must have a clear goal in mind, then make a plan to reach that goal and keep focusing on it and taking the steps that will lead you to it. It doesn't have to be huge, gigantic steps. Consistent, small steps will lead you to it. And Chad, if you believe you have enough time to volunteer, then set that time aside to help others by sharing what you know and what you're good at—after taking care of your personal responsibilities first, of course. Have faith in your ability."

Faith ... there goes that word again. Momma P uses it all the time.

Before Chad leaves, he stops by the door. "Oh, please don't forget my letter of recommendation."

"Yes, I will definitely have one prepared for you. And don't forget to pay close attention to deadlines."

Walking to his next class, Chad replays the conversation he had with Melissa before the guidance counselor intervened and gets angry just thinking about how she was blowing up his phone. *She has a lot of nerve making demands on who she's going to meet. Yeah, get real. Like that's really going to happen.* He snickers to himself.

He runs into Jay on his way to class.

"Hey, CAP, what's going on? Have you been practicing?" Jay asks.

"Nah, not really, to be honest. I know you have though."

"I got mad skills yo. Don't need to practice. Plus with my looks, all the girls are going to be cheering me on," Jay teases.

"You good. No denying that," Chad admits.

"On a serious note, what's going on with you? Lately you've seemed a little agitated."

"It's nothing, just Melissa getting on my nerves."

"Oh, it's girl trouble. Hard to be with them but harder to be without them. But I guess they say the same thing about us, huh?" Jay laughs.

McCorkle

Chad returns the laugh. "For sure."

Questions

Community Service - Offering Your Time

1. Do you think serving your community is important? Why or why not?

2. If you could, what services would you provide for your community?

3. List some programs needed in your community.

4. Are there ways now in which you can volunteer in your community? Name a few.

CHAPTER 12

Lose My Number!

It's Friday evening, and the movie theater is buzzing with moviegoers. An anticipated movie sequel that has everybody talking starts today. Chad is behind the concession stand, looking at a long line of customers waiting to place their order. Holding to their word, he sees his entire family in line as well. To say he's mortified by the sight before him is an understatement.

Poppa P looks like a total misfit. He has nerve to be standing proudly with that huge orange bag in his hand like he just came from trick-or-treating. Potato chips and pretzels sticking out of the bag. And dressed like he's still in the fifties, Chad thinks while shaking his head. Poppa P has on brown polyester pants—tight on top, flare at the bottom—an orange-burgundy-and-green plaid shirt and a tie decorated with burgundy and orange leaves. *Why is he wearing that shirt? It looks like Momma P's Thanksgiving tablecloth,* he wonders.

When they finally get to the counter to place their order, Momma P and his mother make a big deal about the fact that their baby boy works here. Chad is totally embarrassed and asks them to keep it down.

Poppa P says, "I don't know why you're ordering food when I have a bag full of goodies." He holds up the bag for emphasis.

"I don't know why you're being cheap," Momma P snaps.

"It's called being frugal. There's a difference. Being frugal is the way to get ahead financially. A penny saved is a penny earned."

Chad laughs to keep from crying. *Poppa P is always finding ways to save a dollar.*

They ignore Poppa P and look up at the menu. No one is comfortable walking with him, not with the big bag of chips sticking out of his big orange bag. Chad's parents already made plans to walk in front of him when they got to the entrance area.

Momma P rolls her eyes and says, "You look ridiculous with that bright bag of junk food, knowing full darn well you can more than afford to buy the food in here."

"I know I can. But I'm not."

After Chad's mother places her order, a disgruntled Momma P calls out, "Wait, I want something too." She shoots a glare at Poppa P. Chad knows she doesn't indulge in movie-theater food, but she clearly wants to get under Poppa P's skin. She looks up at the menu. "Um … um …" Chad is waiting, giving his grandmother a disbelieving look. "Um … um."

"Momma P, we don't serve 'ums,'" Chad says impatiently.

"Learn to be more patient with the customers." Momma P rolls her eyes and takes another second before she says, "I would like a pack of goobers … some M&Ms with peanuts, oh … Would you like to share a box of Whoppers with me?" she asks Chad's mother. Before she can respond, Momma P says, "And a small soda with a hot dog."

Poppa P interjects, "I thought you said you were on some kind of new diet." He snorts. "It must be new. Never heard of a diet that allows you to eat that much sugar."

"Well, I'm off today, and just for that, make that two hot dogs."

"That's your waistline, not mine." Chad is taking the order and laughing inside. He knows his grandmother isn't really going to eat all that and is just trying to tick Poppa P off. While Chad busies himself with preparing the order, his dad offers him a ride home later when his shift ends.

"No, he doesn't need a ride home," Poppa P says. "The bus stop is right out in front. Public transportation never hurt nobody."

I don't want to be seen with you anyway. You look a mess. Chad gives his grandfather an annoyed look. "No thanks. I'm cool, *Dad.* I'm working a few extra hours tonight anyway." To annoy his grandfather more, Chad says, "Momma P, the funnel cakes are great. You and Mom should try one."

"Okay, baby, I think I will. Me and your mother can share."

"No, it's best if *each* of you had your own." Looking at Poppa P and smirking, he thinks, *I can't wait to see his face when he hears the total.* "Your total is …"

Chad is on break, sitting at a back table and laughing while deep in conversation with a coworker, when Melissa walks in with her friend. Chad notices her first and tries to look down so he won't have to make eye contact. It's too late. Melissa has already seen Chad sitting with a girl.

Melissa stops her friend, nodding in Chad's direction. *Oh boy*, says the look on her friend's face. Melissa stands there for a moment, fuming, studying their body language.

I know my eyes aren't deceiving me, she thinks. *Over there, laughing it up with a girl. They are a little too close and cozy for me. I bet that's that Addison chick. Always talking about how he's busy at work. He doesn't look busy to me. Just look at him over there. Whatever she's saying got him grinning like a goof ball. How dare he be cozying it up with another girl. He gets jealous when I talk with another guy for more than five minutes.* Melissa is getting madder by the second. *And that fool has the nerve to pretend like he doesn't see me.*

"Come on. It's about to be on," she says to her friend.

Walking toward them, Melissa can't see the girl's face because her back is turned toward the door. Arriving at the table, anger temporarily tucked in, Melissa embraces Chad with a huge hug and a wet kiss. Assuming the girl is Addison, she looks the girl up and down. *Dang she's cute.*

With a mocking voice, Melissa says to the girl, "Shouldn't you be making funnel cakes or something?"

"What! What did you just say?"

Chad quickly interjects before something pops off. Chad hates to be between two arguing girls. Before he can break the girls apart, the manager sweeps in accusingly and asks, "Is there a problem over here, Chad?"

"There's about to be," Melissa says. Chad grabs Melissa's arm and speed-walks her to the other side of the theater, out of earshot.

"Come on, Melissa, was that necessary? You about to cause a scene up in here. You know I need this job."

"You *don't* need this job. You *want* this job to be with her over there," Melissa snaps.

Clearly frustrated, Chad says, "What are you talking about? Listen, I can't afford to lose this job. I have bills to pay. Plus, I want to pay my dad back."

Totally ignoring him, she asks, "Are you dating someone else?"

"Dating who?"

"Her, over there." She points. Chad looks in the direction Melissa is pointing, then turns his head back to face her.

"No, we just work together."

"Yeah, whatever. It looked like more than working buddies from where I stood," Melissa accuses.

"Your imagination is running wild. Got you acting all crazy. Isn't your movie about to start?" Chad says, hoping to end the conversation. He needs time to think.

Melissa's friend, previously avoiding the conflict, takes this opportunity to walk over and say, "Girl, we better get going and find some seats. The movie is about to start."

Chad agrees and tells them his break is almost over. He pulls Melissa into an embrace and gives her a juicy, reassuring kiss before dismissing himself. He waits until Melissa has walked into the theater before breathing a sigh of relief. *That was close*, he thinks, standing there and making sure she doesn't go back over to the table. The manager is standing to the side, writing in his notepad.

A few weeks later, Melissa is in her room, sulking. A bored and sad weekend awaits her. Her friends plan to hit a popular eatery that plays music on Friday nights, but Melissa turned down the invite, claiming a headache. She doesn't want to tell them that all she wants to do is curl up in bed—fetal position, earbuds in—and listen to her favorite song while immersing herself in thoughts of Chad. Even her dad couldn't get her to come over for the weekend, and she loves spending time with him.

For the past few days, she's been heartbroken and occupied by thoughts of her downhill relationship with Chad. She just can't fathom where it all went wrong. A little before school started back up again, after he came back from visiting his family for summer break, things went awry. And she just can't put her finger on why.

It must be that girl, Addison, he keeps mentioning. I wonder if they were talking for the entire summer while he was away. We used to be inseparable, and now I don't know what happened between us. He changed so much since we first met.

Lying on her bed, she looks at a picture of them on their first date. She keeps it on her dresser. Those were happier, fun times. With a broken heart and a million questions, she stares at the picture and says aloud, "What happened to us? How did we get here?" Tears fall down her cheeks as she reminisces about the first time she laid eyes on him and their first date.

She was sitting in class waiting for it to start, when right before the bell rings, Chad swaggered in with his book bag over his shoulder. His presence demands attention. And he gets it from Melissa and a few other females. While he is walking to an empty seat, their eyes connect. A kind of I'm-checking-you-out stare.

From that day, Melissa is attracted to him, and him to her, but he doesn't try to get to know Melissa right after that, and she never has the courage to approach him.

One day during lunch, Chad is rapping in the cafeteria. After his mediocre performance, she finally approaches him to pay him a compliment, saying he is great, when deep down she knows he isn't. His looks more than compensate for his inadequate rapping skills. He smiles and thanks her. From that day forward, they start talking casually and getting to know each other. After a few weeks, he asks her out on a date, and she accepts, wondering what took him so long.

Their first date starts with breakfast at the Pancake House. It is the most romantic date of her life. Chad is the perfect gentlemen. The entire day he treats her like a queen, like her dad and mom said she should be treated. He even brings her half a dozen roses.

After that, they go out countless times. He opens doors for her and performs other pleasing acts of kindness. Each date is more fun than the last. He keeps her laughing. He even writes two poems for her that he frames as a gift. He is good at writing poetry. Their only arguments are debates about who is the best rapper.

They shared their dreams and found they had a lot in common. His dream was to become a rich rapper, and hers was to become a famous TV personality.

"I thought we were going to be the next big power couple," she says to herself, returning from memory lane. *I should've never allowed him into my world. It was peaceful before him.* She picks up a pillow and throws it at the dresser, knocking the picture and the framed poems to the floor. She's mad and torn at the same time. She feels about ready to explode. "Forget him," she says as if someone can hear her.

She calls up her friends and tells them the change in plans. She will be joining them after all. She gets dressed in her fitted designer jeans. Taking into account her small breasts, she chooses a shirt that accentuates her flat stomach. Going into her makeup box, she digs out foundation to cover the blemishes on her face. Satisfied with her handy work, she adorns her eyelids with a shimmery eyeshadow that complements her hazel eyes before lathering her lips with strawberry-flavored lip gloss. She puts on a pair of riding boots, grabs her bag, and gives herself a once-over in the mirror.

She picks up her keys and cell phone, which starts to ring in her hand. A smile forms on her face after looking at the screen.

"Yes! I knew he couldn't stay away from me for too long," she says. Trying her best not to sound happy, she changes her voice. "What is it, Chad? I'm in a rush, heading out the—" She stops midsentence. "Hello ... Hello ... Chad ... Chad!" Melissa doesn't get an answer but hears voices in the background, including Chad's; he's telling somebody he's going on lunch break and will be back in forty-five minutes. After a minute of listening, she hangs up.

Evidently he called me by accident.

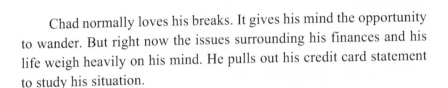

Chad normally loves his breaks. It gives his mind the opportunity to wander. But right now the issues surrounding his finances and his life weigh heavily on his mind. He pulls out his credit card statement to study his situation.

Knowing it's a good time to talk since he's on lunch break, Melissa calls Chad back exactly ten minutes later. Putting down the statement, he answers, distracted.

"Hey, what are you doing?" she asks.

"Working," he answers. She doesn't let on that she knows he's on break.

"Can you talk?"

"Nah, not right now. I'm busy, but I will call you back when I get off, okay?" he says smoothly.

To make sure she heard correctly, she asks, "When is your break? Maybe I will walk over and keep you company."

"I took it already."

Bingo, that lying dog, she thinks. *Okay, let's see how slick he thinks he is.* "Busy doing what?"

"What's up with the questions, Melissa?" Chad frowns into the phone.

"What do you mean, what's up with the questions? What ... you with that girl, Addison, or something? If I catch—"

He cuts her off midsentence. "Mel, you tripping, and I don't have time to argue with you. You know I'm at work, taking care of business. I don't need the stress or the distraction right now. Plus, the manager is looking dead at me, talking on the phone. I'll talk to you later." Without waiting for a response, Chad disconnects the line.

In her mind the lie speaks volumes. It fills her insides with anger and inflames her hunger for a fight. Totally forgetting about meeting up with her girlfriends, she quickly tears off her clothes and changes into a pair of sweats and sneakers. Snatching her hair back into a ponytail, she storms out of the house, ready for war. She imagines Chad smooching Addison in a corner of the theater.

I know she's in his face, giving him some type of advice. Putting her two cents in where it's not needed. Chad thinks this chick is the next bright thing since the sun. Just like I caught them together the other day, and he's got the nerve to say my imagination is running wild. I'm going to show them whose imagination is running wild, and this time the manager will not be able to stop me. I don't care if he gets fired. It will serve him right. He needs to be working on his lyrics for the competition anyway, she thinks while dreams of becoming a power couple drift out the window.

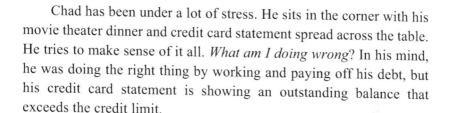

Chad has been under a lot of stress. He sits in the corner with his movie theater dinner and credit card statement spread across the table. He tries to make sense of it all. *What am I doing wrong?* In his mind, he was doing the right thing by working and paying off his debt, but his credit card statement is showing an outstanding balance that exceeds the credit limit.

Account Information		Account Summary	
Statement Closing Date	12/15		
Credit Limit	**1500.00**		
Available Credit	$0.00		
Available Cash	$0.00		
		Previous Balance	$1,400.00
		- Other Credits	$00.00
		+ Purchases	$100.00
		+ Cash Advances	
		+ Other Debits	
		+Late Fee Charged	$25.00
		+ Interest Charged	$24.15
		= New Balance	**$1549.15**

Payment Information

He's totally confused and feels like throwing in the towel. For a fleeting moment, he thinks about Melissa's advice to stop paying the bill altogether, but he quickly dismisses it.

While he reviews the statement with Addison, trying to solve the mystery, the suggestion that he should tell his mother is posed again.

"Your mom could help you figure out what's going on with your bill. The fees showing on the statement are mysterious to you but may not be mysterious to her. She probably has the answers you're looking for."

"No," he says adamantly. "She will solve the problem but then kill me afterward for going over the credit limit."

"What's the difference? The bill is killing you anyway. You're going to have to make a decision pretty soon, because your present plan of action is obviously not working."

Frustrated, Chad agrees. "Yeah, obviously."

"*So,* are you going to tell her?"

"Will you leave me alone with that?" Chad snaps.

"Okay, I will leave you alone. Don't say I didn't warn you."

Just then, Melissa storms into the movie theater, huffing and puffing from her fast-paced walk there. When she gets through the door, she stands in the lobby, searching Chad out. It's hard to see through the weekend crowd of people.

"Excuse me. Pardon me. Sorry," Melissa apologizes as she squeezes through the mob of moviegoers, stopping a few times to ask Chad's coworkers whether they've seen him. "Dang!" Melissa huffs.

A female worker rushing by bumps into Melissa. The young girl, obviously heated about who-knows-what, looks Melissa up and down. A literal up and down, with the head movement included.

Did she just scan me? Melissa thinks.

"Excuse me, but do you know Chad?" Melissa asks her.

"Yeah," she says, obviously not willing to give any more information.

What is her problem? Melissa muses. "Have you seen him around?"

The girl pauses, absorbing the question before answering, "He's in the back, eating."

"Is he still there?"

The girl sucks her teeth. "Yeah, I just left from over there. Check the table in the corner by the window."

"Thank you."

The girl with the attitude walks off without a simple nod. Frozen momentarily in place, Melissa is taken aback by the girl's attitude. Shaking it off and concentrating on the reason she's there, Melissa spots Chad sitting at a table in the exact spot the girl with the nasty attitude said he would be. Arriving at the table, she looks down at him. Hands on hips.

"You lying dog!" Melissa spits.

Chad jumps a little, startled by the sudden outburst breaking his train of thought. He looks up with an exasperated expression. "What … What's up with you, Melissa, and lying about what?"

"I thought you said you were working. Is this part of your job? Sitting down at a table with food in front of you?"

"I *was* working at the time," he admits.

"Liar!" Melissa yells.

Customers are staring now. She looks over at them. "What are you looking at? Mind your own business."

Totally embarrassed, Chad says, "They can't help but stare. You're making it everybody's business."

"Listen. Don't try to change the subject."

"Really? What subject is that? You're not making any sense right now. Seriously, Mel, you need to get a grip. You're starting to tick me off," Chad says, losing his patience.

"I'm starting to tick *you* off! You are unbelievable. You lie to my face and then have the audacity to say *I'm* starting to tick *you* off. Well, guess what? You've already ticked me off."

He grits his teeth and says calmly, "What are you ticked off about now?"

"Your lying, cheating self was not aware that you accidentally called me. When I picked up the phone to say hello, you didn't answer. But I heard you telling somebody that you were taking a forty-five-minute lunch break. I waited ten minutes before I called you back, assuming you would be on break by then. And when I did make an attempt to come be with you, you claimed you were busy and still working."

Chad stares at her for a moment, trying to conjure up something logical to say. "At the time I *was* still working. I didn't take my break right away."

"Chad, I'm going to ask you one time and one time only. And please don't lie to me. Were you having lunch with Addison?"

"And I'm going to tell you one time and one time only. No. I was having lunch by myself. Don't you see food for only one person?"

She looks down at the table. "Yeah, but you could've shared."

"Don't you see one drink?" he persists.

"You could've shared that too!" she yells.

"Come on, Melissa, look. Don't you see one chair over here? And I'm sitting in it."

"Yeah ... well ... you could've shared that too."

Not bothering to respond at first, Chad gives her an incredulous look. "Listen," he says, "I was sitting here, going over my credit card bill, which has me stressed, and you're adding to it."

She calms down a bit as she looks down at the papers on the table. "I thought we discussed this already."

"Yeah, we discussed it. I decided to continue paying my bill every month, but it's still not stopping these mystery fees from appearing. I don't know where they're coming from.

Late fee: $25.00
Interest fee: $24.15

"I don't know why the bank is charging me fees when I'm paying the bill every month like they asked. The bill is *still* going up. This has got me vexed right now ... for real."

"Well, obviously the card is rigged, or they're stealing your money or something. Like I keep telling you, just stop paying," Melissa suggests.

"I can't do that!"

"Why not?" Melissa asks. "You just said you pay your bill each month, and the bill still goes up without you using it. You're just wasting your money."

"Because I owe them, that's why. Besides, my mom told me something about not paying your bills having a negative effect on your FICO score. And I'm trying to keep it 700."

"Fi what?" Melissa asks, confused.

"My FICO score," Chad answers. "Listen, I can't explain right now, so just forget it." He pauses to look up at her. "I used their money, and it's only right I pay them back. Just like it's right to pay my dad back for the money he gave me for the car."

"I understand why you want to pay your dad back, but with this credit card business, it looks like your honesty isn't getting you nowhere but a bigger balance and a headache that I feel you're taking out on me," Melissa says with an attitude.

"This isn't about you, Mel. Why do you have to make everything about you? I'm not taking this out on you. There you go with your wild imagination again."

"I'm going to pretend I didn't hear that. Listen, I don't know what else to tell you. Stop paying them, is all I can say."

"Yeah, figures," Chad says while shaking his head.

"What's that supposed to mean?"

"Whatever definition you make up," Chad says smartly.

"You see, that's what I'm talking about. There you go taking it out on me."

"I'm not taking it out on you, but the solutions you are giving me are stupid. You didn't mind me using the card buying things for you, and the smartest thing you can think of is to stop paying."

"Hold up." Melissa throws her hand up in the air.

"No. *You* hold up," Chad says. "Just like when I complained to you about my manager, your solution was to quit. How was that going to resolve my bills and my debt to my dad?"

"Who do you think—"

Chad cuts her off again, already knowing what she's going to ask. "You. I'm talking to you. The only thing you are concerned with is the rapping competition and getting a spot on TV. Like I said, it's all about you. And I'm starting to question if it was ever about me and what I wanted."

"Can I talk now?" Melissa demands.

"Only if you have something to say that makes sense. Until I figure out what's going on with my credit card bill and solve this mystery, I'm not feeling anything else you have to say."

Melissa gives him an incredulous look. "I know you don't think you just dismissed me."

"I just did. You're getting a little clingy anyway, showing up at my job for no other reason but to stalk me."

Deeply hurt, Melissa whispers, "Clingy ... really ... Okay, that's cool. Since I'm so clingy and acting all stalker-ish, I'm going to un-cling myself. You and that Addison chick can have each other. Let *her* help you solve the case of the mystery fees. I'm quite sure she will have a *smart* resolution. I'm done!"

She knocks over his papers and food, and storms off, leaving Chad to clean it up, including the now-messy credit card statement. "See, that's what I'm talking about. Bright, just bright," he mumbles while wiping the glob of food off his papers.

A few days after the argument, Melissa still won't accept Chad's apology. After calming down, he realized he was too harsh with her and desperately wants to make amends. He knows it's not fair to blame his issues on Melissa. He remembers what his grandfather told him. *"A man takes full responsibility for his own mistakes."* And that's what he intends to do.

For starters he wants to reach out to Melissa. He misses her badly and didn't realize how much he loved her until she discarded him like expired milk. In school he makes every attempt to approach her, but as soon as he does, she makes a scene and tells him to get away from her. He even tries going to her house, but each time her mother says she isn't home.

He talks with Addison about his breakup with Melissa.

"Maybe the separation is a good thing," Addison says.

"What's so good about it?" he argues.

"For one, so you and I … can concentrate on getting your debt in order without distractions. Once we solve the mystery fees, you can work on trying to get her back." After a pause, Addison adds, "That's if she takes you back."

"By that time it may be too late," he says with a worried tone.

"Don't worry. If it's meant to be, it will be. If not, you always have me."

Together they try to crack the case of the mysterious fees. Addison again suggests that he tell his mother, positive that she would have a solution. Chad still refuses to take heed, halfheartedly believing Addison isn't always right.

Weeks go by, and as hard as Chad tries to concentrate on his bills, Melissa still invades his bruised heart.

"I tried everything. How do you think I can get Melissa back?" he blurts to Addison while they're going over his bills.

"I thought you said we were going to solve your financial problem before getting back with her."

"No. That's what *you* said," Chad says.

"And I thought we agreed."

"If we did, I can still change my mind. And that's what I'm doing. Exercising my free will," Chad says.

"You need to exercise that same free will and tell your momma about those fees that are piling up."

"Let me worry about that," Chad stubbornly says.

"Okay, but don't come whining to me when Melissa starts getting on your nerves again."

"How can I get Melissa and me on the same page and let her know the dreams she has for me aren't who I am?"

"For one, by being honest with yourself. Stop pretending to be someone you're not. Then be honest with her. And that includes telling her about me. Let her know *I'm not* going anywhere. You and I have a special connection."

Chad's brow furrows. "I can't tell her about us. That's crazy."

"The only reason Melissa is stressing you out now is because you see your reflection in her actions. At one point you two were just alike: both obsessed with money, fame, and material things. Now that you see where that got you, buried in debt, you want to change. But remember, Melissa is still the same person you met. You can't get mad at her because you made a detour on the road you both were traveling on. You changed without giving her notice. Everything you learned along the way, teach her. Maybe that will help her to see your point of view and inspire her to change too."

Chad argues, "She can be stubborn. She probably won't listen."

"Don't be so quick to judge. Let me remind you that your attitude toward certain things in life was the same as hers not too long ago. Her interests that now annoy you are what you both had in common before."

He relents. "Yeah, maybe I will sit down with her and come clean. Tell her everything that's going on with me, minus you. I don't want to lose her, and you definitely aren't going anywhere."

He takes Addison's advice that evening and makes another attempt to go to Melissa's house, this time with roses he purchased for her mother, hoping to soften the situation.

On his way to Melissa's, he goes on Facebook. He hasn't been on social media in a while, all too occupied with more important matters. Scrolling through Melissa's timeline, he discovers alarming posts. One says, "Mom would like to know about that financial situation. I'm thinking about telling her."

Chad knows instantly what she's referring to. Shocked that she would stoop so low, he gets off at the next bus stop and leaves the roses in an empty seat, ignoring the strange stares from other passengers. During their separation, Melissa has been spending her time on social media, posting camouflaged threats about Chad's financial situation only he can decipher. After making the trek back home, Chad calls Melissa, and the call goes straight to voice mail. He follows up with a text message.

"Yo r u threatening me?! looked at your page. y would u post that?"

After a few seconds, his phone vibrates with a text from Melissa. "What r u talking about?"

"Don't play stupid with me. I caught those messages on social media," Chad texts back.

"I still don't know what ur talkin about." His phone vibrates in the middle of him texting back. "I can post whatever I want!"

Getting angrier by the minute, Chad texts, "U r crossin a line of no return."

"Is that a threat?"

"Uv been warned!!" Chad texts.

"N guess what? So have u!!? So when yr mother give you a beat down 4 maxin out that credit line, don't say I didn't warn u! LOSE MY #, LOSER!"

"Consider it lost," Chad texts back.

The next evening, Chad contemplates his next move and the text message feud between him and Melissa while riding on the bus from work. Sitting in the back near a window, earbuds in, his thoughts flip back and forth between his finances and Melissa's threats. Thinking about her posts on social media, he becomes angry.

Cruising on the bus, Chad stares out the tinted window, exploring the world in search for something interesting, anything that will take his mind to another space. He looks down on the passing pedestrians, the stores, and the cars until finally his eyes settle on his reflection. Not liking what he sees, he mumbles to himself, "What's wrong with you? What was I thinking trying to make up with that … that little snitch!"

In a state of disbelief at Melissa's threat to reveal his financial secret, Chad sits and ponders the idea to tell his mother before Melissa does, but soon dismisses it. His attempts to apologize to Melissa are futile, and he questions her loyalty. Before arriving at his stop, he concludes that time away from Melissa will help him to concentrate on the issues he needs to resolve.

CHAPTER 13

Integrity

In the following weeks, Chad works on getting his financial issues in order. He speaks with his parents about college and the FASFA forms, and together they complete the required forms and apply for college loans. He tries to keep up with his studies and maintain an acceptable grade point average. He fills out college applications, wishing he was able to put down volunteering as a way of giving back to the community, but his long hours at work take up all his time. He collects letters of recommendation from a few teachers and his guidance counselor. At work he tries his best to have patience with the rude customers but finds it difficult, so he asks Momma P to pray for him. She does but tells him to pray for himself as well. He does.

Melissa continues to blast Chad on social media, airing her frustrations and celebrating her singlehood so the world can see. Every so often, Chad goes on social media, sees her messages, and tries his best to keep the anger from boiling over. He thinks it's stupid of her to tell their business to the world. He doesn't see what purpose it serves. She has sent out several threats to call his mom, but so far she hasn't executed any of them.

"Single lady about 2 text momma a 1K prize. Wish I could be there 2 c her surprise." Chad isn't the least bit worried. Melissa is just blowing smoke; she doesn't have his mother's number, or so he thinks. But he soon finds out how serious Melissa is when she pastes part of his mother's number on social media as a warning. This is the final straw.

He makes plans to pay her an unexpected visit when he gets off work.

After two knocks, Melissa's mother opens the door.

"Hi, Ms. Tanya, is Melissa home?"

"Come on in. Have a seat. I'll get her for you." Melissa's mother gives him a pitying smile as she goes into the other room. After a moment, she gives him permission to go in Melissa's bedroom. "Make sure you leave that door cracked. Wide!"

Walking into the bedroom like a baby taking his first steps, he awkwardly says, "Hey." The bus ride to her apartment provided some time for his anger to simmer down.

"Hey. What you standing there for? If you have something to say, say it. Or leave the same way you came," Melissa pouts.

Chad blurts, "What's up with you? Posting those stupid threats on social media. Who goes around snitching to mothers?"

"I do. And what about it?" Melissa snaps.

"Listen, I know you may be upset about our situation, but I would never snitch on you, *especially* to your mother. So that's how you going to be. What happened to trust?"

"Trust!" she repeats. "Are you for real? What happens to trust when you're in Addison's face, huh? Don't talk to me about trust!"

He gives her an unimpressed stare. "You reaped some of the benefits from that credit card, and you gonna stand there and threaten to tell my mother about the high balance all because of your insecurities and a vendetta against someone you don't know."

"I am not insecure!" Melissa yells.

"Yes, you are. You think I don't catch on when you compare yourself to other girls and say hateful things about them to make yourself feel better."

She was stunned beyond belief, hurt that his words resonated. It felt like a sharp object cutting deep. She opened her mouth, but the words got caught in her throat. A quick response wasn't forthcoming. Hurt quickly turned to fury. *How could he?* she thinks.

"First of all, I'm not threatened by *any* girl! And second of all, how do you expect me to feel when you keep mentioning all the good advice Addison gives you? I find that totally disrespectful. And third of all, I am not insecure." she almost shouts.

"Is everything all right in there?" Melissa's mother yells from down the hall.

"Yes!" they both shout simultaneously.

Chad opens his mouth to say something but quickly shuts it again. He stares into space, his eyes fixed on something she can't see.

He's reminded of the possible consequences that will arise from being dishonest with himself and Melissa. He directs his stare at Melissa; her expression conveys that she wants an immediate apology. Humbling himself, he walks over to her bed and sits down. "Listen, Mel, I was an idiot. And I'm sorry. I was wrong for how I was acting, but I was under a lot of pressure, and you weren't being supportive of the changes I was going through. Addison only offers advice when I need it. It's nothing you have to worry about. That's all. And it was pretty decent advice, even though I didn't listen to it all the time."

"But—" she interrupts.

"Wait, let me finish. There's no reason to be jealous just because the advice happens to come from another place. My place is here with you. You don't have to worry about Addison. I love *you*."

"But it's still no excuse for you acting like a donkey," she sulks.

"I know." He pauses and then blurts out, "I don't want to be a rapper! I don't mind writing poetry, but I have to be honest. I don't want to be a rapper and perform on stage. I just like writing poetry. Either you need to accept me for who I am and stop pressuring me, or I'm going to have to … never mind." Melissa gives him a look. "Listen, just please stop asking me about the rap competition. I'm not entering. Period. I suck at rapping."

"No, you—"

Chad cuts Melissa off. "Stop. Yes, I do. And you need to stop lying. You know you just want to catch a spot on TV." She keeps quiet. The look on her face confirms he's right. "It's all good. At one time it was both of our dreams, but it's not mine anymore. I want to do other things, like write poetry, get serious about my college apps, save money, buy a car, and stop spending money like I got it like that, because I don't. I will one day. But right now I don't. And I'm cool with that. Oh … and I finally know what I want to do in the future. I want to major in accounting."

"Really."

"Yeah, you know I like math and numbers and stuff, but I realized finance and accounting are something I may be interested in when I started having problems with my credit card. I'm determined to figure out what's going on with the continuous increases on my credit card bill."

"I already told you what—"

He throws his hand up. "Please."

Her heart is now light. Melissa feels as if she can breathe again now that they are on better terms. She has been missing him like crazy. "You know you aren't the only who has been making some changes. I looked into getting a job. My friend said it's guaranteed I'll get it. She's cool with the manager, plus they're hiring."

"That's cool," Chad says, feeling happy for her.

"Yeah, I think so too, and when I start getting paid, I'm going to help you start paying that credit card bill, but first you better figure out why your bill keeps going up because I'm not throwing my money away. You know what?" she says as if just receiving a solution to his problems. "You pay your bill, and the balance goes up, so maybe if you don't pay your bill, the balance may go down."

"I'm afraid to ask, but I am anyway. Are you serious?"

"I'm joking, but listen, I'm trying to help you out. You can't seem to figure it out. So I think you better ask your mom. Just take your licking and keep on ticking."

"Do you want to take it for me?" he kids.

"Heck no … I love you but not that much."

Chad laughs; it seems like he hasn't laughed in forever. "You're crazy. But seriously, you don't have to help me pay that bill."

"I want to. That's what power couples do." She leans in. "Now shut up. I'm dying for a kiss." She pulls her lips away briefly to say,

"Oh, and for the record, I wasn't going to tell your mom. I was just angry and saying those things to get under your skin."

"I should hope not, because you know snitches get stitches, right?" he jokes.

"Yeah, okay." She nudges the side of his head.

"Oh ... and I'm sorry about what I said about you being insecure," he says remorsefully.

"Apology accepted. Since we are being honest, I do feel bad about my breast size. I wish I had bigger boobs. Is there enough on your credit card to charge me a larger pair?" They both laugh. "But seriously, it's not that I be hating on other girls. I just wish I was 2 cups bigger in the breast department."

"I like you just the way you are. But at the end of the day it's not about me and what I like. It's about being confident with whatever God gave you."

"Ooookaaay! I know that line didn't just come from you. Did that come from Addison too?" she asks with raised eyebrows.

He smiles and admits, "No ... that actually came from my grandmother."

"Smart woman." Melissa smiles.

Chad returns her smile. "She a'ight."

CHAPTER 14

Managing Credit

Two nights later, as Chad lies in bed, he looks for some sign to tell him what to do. He doesn't know what that something would be. He feels troubled and needs some answers. Never has he felt so unhinged, or at least he never noticed it before. He feels lost and frustrated. Right before falling asleep, he decides he has had enough.

"I know I should do the right thing, but it's too much work. I'm not up for this." He yawns. "I don't care what Melissa says. I'm not telling my mother."

Chad shifts his body. As he falls into a fitful sleep, his dark dreams soon follow.

He is sitting in an office, his desk swarmed with papers. Sitting across from him is a couple. They are elated. "Thank you. Thank you so much for showing us how to improve our credit. Now we can start planning for the home we always dreamed of purchasing. Your manager said we were in good hands. And you proved it."

"No problem. I'm glad I could be of service," Chad says, happy he has an internship at a bank where he can positively impact people's financial lives. "Once I get the approval from my manager, I will send you a copy."

Chad heads out the door with them. He's on his way to meet Melissa for a date. He strolls down the street, feeling at peace and looking forward to a fun-filled evening. The sun is out, and the trees are full and lush. People walking by seem to be enjoying the weather.

Passing a flower shop, he stops in to pick out tulips for Melissa. He makes his purchase and tells the guy at the counter to keep the change.

"Do you have the time?" he asks the clerk.

"Yeah, it's five ten." The clerk snickers.

What's so funny? Chad muses.

"Thanks." As Chad exits the floral shop, he notices the instant change in the weather. It has become cloudy. It begins to drizzle. He opens his umbrella to protect the flowers and continues on his way. In the blink of an eye, the drizzle turns into a downpour, and everyone is running for shelter. The downpour doesn't spoil his mood. He strolls up the block, turning the corner onto Giving Up Avenue. He cuts through the park and heads toward the train station, but as his footsteps echo through the park, he gets the sudden feeling of being very alone. *Dang, where did everybody go?* His body jerks as a passerby bumps him.

"Hey, watch where you're going," Chad calls out to the tall, impeccably dressed man. The man ignores him and continues running, disappearing into the train station. Chad quickens his pace. Umbrella held down low, obstructing his view, he tries to prevent himself from becoming soaked. As he gets to the stairs of the train station, he bumps into something. He lifts his umbrella to see what he's bumped into, and his breath catches in his throat. Standing right in front of him is a villian with a hatchet.

Chad backs away and makes a beeline in the direction he came, but now it's pitch black outside. The park has turned into woods with monstrous trees swaying everywhere from the thundering storm. He runs, gasping for breath. It's difficult because he can't see a thing in front of him through the blackness. Another villian jumps out from behind a tree.

He snarls, "Hey you ... 510, where do you think you're going? You belong to me."

"My name isn't 510," Chad whimpers.

"Come here, 510," he yells with an angry snarl. "I'm going to bury you alive. I prepared a five-foot, ten-inch hole just for you." Hearing that, Chad picks up speed, running for his life, only to be slowed down by his stumbling feet. He looks down to see what's slowing him, and it's Ms. Mystery Fee sticking out her designer-clad foot to purposefully trip him up. He keeps pushing on, panting and sweating. The more he tries to get away from the villains, the more Ms. Mystery Fee sticks her foot out. Everywhere he runs, that designer-clad foot is there to trip him up. Chest tightening and unable to see, he presses on to find his way through the thick, dark, and heavy rain.

His feet move him toward a hole prepared for him. Out comes the designer-clad foot to trip him up again. He trips and falls into the hole, barely grabbing onto the rocky edge. His feet are dangling, and he's yelling for help, desperately hanging on with the tips of his fingers. Out of the pitch black, a flash of lightning floods the area with light for two seconds, revealing a pair of shoes worn by a dark figure.

Boom! Another flash of lightning reveals the dark figure to be the well-dressed man who bumped into him earlier. His piercing eyes gleam below heavy brows, and he's glaring at Chad. Chad gasps loudly and jerks his head back, almost causing him to lose his grip. The pounding of his heart blends with the thunder.

The man squats down and says, "Take my hand!" Chad, too afraid of falling, refuses. "Trust me. Let go! Release one hand. I got you."

Chad struggles with the decision; he's afraid to move. The man notices Chad's conflict and says, "If you continue to hold on as you are, you won't make it—" His words are cut off when one of the villains throws a punch to the back of the man's head. Stumbling from the blow, he shouts again to Chad. "Come on, you can do it. Trust me. Take my hand!"

Chad musters up the courage and extends one of his hands to the man. His other hand is shaking, barely able to sustain his weight. Sweat drips down his face mixing with tears of anguish. His fingers are losing their grip while his rescuer fights off his foes. First is the pinky, then the thumb, leaving only three fingers left holding on. Unable to keep his grip any longer, his last three fingers slip. In that exact instant, Chad's body is yanked up.

Chad is pulled to his feet. Set on solid ground, he wobbles in his sneakers, still unsteady. Soon after catching his breath, someone grabs his shoulders and spins him around. The villains are leering at him, all with green eyes, preparing to pounce—snarling and grunting. Ms. Mystery Fee sexily smiling, satisfied she's cornered her prey.

The villains yell, "We have to bury the present and the future for good this time!" Because of his rescuer, Chad has mustered up enough courage to fight back. Together they fight, taking the enemies down one by one. The villains surrender and form a truce with the more powerful duo. Chad's victory creates an alliance that stills the storm and brings out the sun with a ray of bright light.

His newfound comrades introduce themselves, more politely this time.

"I'm Mr. FICO, here to serve your greatest need, sir."

Taking a bow, another one says in a deep guttural voice, "I'm FAFSA, always at your service. And the sexy one over there," he points, "is Fee."

"That's 'Ms. Fee' to you, shuga!" She winks, then continues in a honeyed tone. "I'm misunderstood. Scary to many but necessary for those rendering services. I'm quite indispensable, you know." She bats her alluring green eyes. Chad eyes her, keeping his guard up. He finds her alluring and interesting at the same time. He wants to get acquainted and understand her better. A lazy smile creeps across his face. He's growing a smidgen more comfortable. Upon closer inspection, he finds her attractive. Taking cautious steps, he moves in closer.

Boom! Loud thunder breaks his stride. Chad screams the loudest his lungs can manage, "Momma!"

He wakes to find himself soaked and rolling in sweat. *That was crazy. I'm sick of these nightmares*, he muses.

He takes a shower and changes his sheets, all the while deciding how to tell his mother about his financial situation. While waiting for his mother to get home from work, he goes to his drawer and pulls out all his previous statements, including the most recent one. Chad takes another stab at trying to understand the accumulating fees on his statement, but they only make him frustrated and sleepy. He falls back to sleep with a pile of statements on his chest.

"Addison! Addison!" His mother yells.

He awakes, startled. A few hours have passed, and his mother is standing over him, waving papers in her hand. Not giving him a chance to collect his bearings, she yells, "Get dressed and meet me in the kitchen. Now!" Without saying another word, she storms out the door. Chad is left staring at her back.

She doesn't give him a chance to respond. He doesn't want to.

Hearing her shout his middle name is a warning to keep his mouth shut. His mother only calls him Addison when she's annoyed about something he did. His mind races. *I knew I should've told her. It's about to be on.*

When Chad gets downstairs, Poppa and Momma P are at the table, putting a puzzle together and arguing about which pieces go where.

"What is this?" Nicole immediately starts in on him.

"I know what you're thinking." He looks at her frowning expression and says, "Maybe I don't know what you're thinking, but I can explain. As you can see, I'm paying the bill every month, but the amount I submit isn't being totally deducted from the outstanding balance. If I send in thirty dollars, the bank only deducts six dollars from my balance. I don't know what they're doing with the other twenty-four dollars! And I don't know where all these fees came from. It's like a mystery." He sighs, exasperated. "You need to call the bank, Mom, and tell them this credit card is rigged or something."

"You need to call the doctor and tell 'em his head is rigged," Poppa P announces.

Nicole shoots him a look. "Poppa P, this isn't a joking matter."

"It wasn't meant to be a joke," Poppa P responds.

"Sit down," she says.

Chad takes a seat at the table, making sure not to get too close to his mother. She moves closer to Chad and points to the fees and interest the bank charged for his minimum-only payments. His mother takes a look at his previous statements and notices a lot of charges for sneakers. "Addison, I can't believe this. You maxed out your credit card for purchases mainly on sneakers."

Shaking his head, Poppa P interjects, "Um … um … um … you're in debt … for *sneakers*! That's a shame. That money could've been invested in a sneaker company or some other business."

Chad stares at the balance in dismay. "I'll never be able to pay this bill off."

"Yes, you will," Nicole says. "You are going to pay back every cent, including the money your dad gave you for a car. I'm going to make sure of that. You should've told me what was going on instead of keeping this to yourself."

"I was trying to take care of it myself," Chad says.

"Yeah, but where did that get you?" she asks.

Poppa P looks over their shoulders, staring down at the bill.

Upset, Nicole turns her head slightly, raising the statement in the air, and asks, "Does this have your name on it?"

"No. But the deed to this house does," Poppa snaps.

Nicole sighs. "Unless you are going to make a contribution to this bill, I can take it from here. Thank you."

"Hold up! Hold up, little girl. I did make a contribution. My knowledge is what I contributed, but you didn't take it, and that's why you're in this predicament. I told his father that Chad didn't need a car, that there is nothing wrong with public transportation. Just a little dirt … stank smell … a mob of bodies…."

Nicole lets out an exasperated sigh. "Are you done?"

"No. Rats, pole dancers, panhandlers, band players, singers, preachers, and loud-talking students which never hurt nobody. And I told you," he said, pointing to Nicole for emphasis, "not to get him a credit card because he's still being controlled, manipulated, and economically stripped by social media and advertisement. That he wouldn't be ready for one until he came out from under their influence. But noooo! Nobody listens to me around here." Before he turns his attention back to the puzzle, he says, "Oh yeah, and next time watch your tone before you *and* your family find yourself on the opposite side of that door."

Nicole gives Poppa P an apologetic look and humbly turns her attention back to Chad. "You do see the interest the bank is charging you for *only* paying the minimum in addition to the late fees, right?"

"But you never explained that part to me when you gave me the card," Chad says in his defense.

Momma P looks at Nicole with a smirk on her face. She chimes in, "Well, he got a point. When someone is given the responsibility of having a credit card, it's important to explain *everything* to them to avoid financial mishaps like this one." She scoots over and says, "This is the part your mother left out when she gave you the card, and that's why you're confused about these fees. Fees aren't a mystery. Baby, they're only a mystery when you don't understand them and don't ask questions."

"Momma P, if I would've known, I wouldn't be in this predicament," Chad says, glad he has someone on his side.

"Now slow down, young man. I'm not saying this is entirely your mother's fault, but she is *partially* to blame. However, you aren't totally off the hook. She did explain how paying your credit card bills late negatively affect your FICO score and your credit history."

"Sure did ... I heard her," Poppa P says.

"Well, I'm going to explain it again." Momma P motions to Chad to lean in. "So going forward, there will be no excuse and no one to blame but yourself if you wreck your personal finances. But first I'm going to explain the fees the creditors are charging you and why your bill is increasing instead of decreasing."

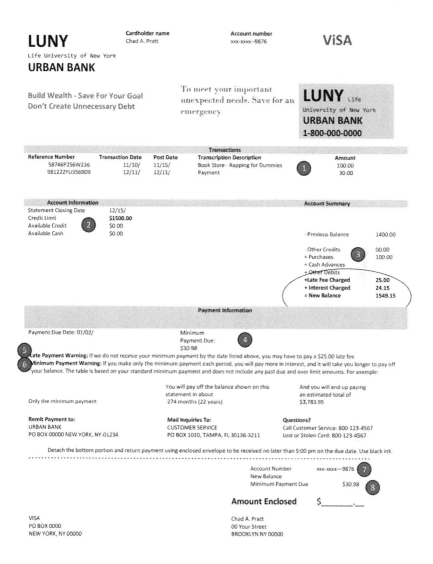

LUNY
Life University of New York
URBAN BANK

Cardholder name
Chad A. Pratt

Account number
xxx-xxxx-9876

ViSA

Build Wealth - Save For Your Goal
Don't Create Unnecessary Debt

To meet your important
unexpected needs. Save for an
emergency

LUNY Life
University of New York
URBAN BANK
1-800-000-0000

Transactions

Reference Number	Transaction Date	Post Date	Transcription Description		Amount
58746P256W236	11/10/	11/15/	Book Store - Rapping for Dummies	1	100.00
981222YU3569D9	12/11/	12/11/	Payment		30.00

Account Information

Statement Closing Date	12/15/
Credit Limit	$1500.00
Available Credit	$0.00
Available Cash	$0.00

(2)

Account Summary

· Previous Balance	1400.00
· Other Credits	00.00
+ Purchases	100.00
+ Cash Advances	
+ Other Debits	
+Late Fee Charged	25.00
+ Interest Charged	24.15
= New Balance	1549.15

(3)

Payment Information

Payment Due Date: 01/02/

Minimum
Payment Due:
$30.98

(4)

Late Payment Warning: If we do not receive your minimum payment by the date listed above, you may have to pay a $25.00 late fee

Minimum Payment Warning: If you make only the minimum payment each period, you will pay more in interest, and it will take you longer to pay off your balance. The table is based on your standard minimum payment and does not include any past due and over limit amounts. For example:

Only the minimum payment	You will pay off the balance shown on this statement in about 274 months (22 years)	And you will end up paying an estimated total of $3,783.95

Remit Payment to:
URBAN BANK
PO BOX 00000 NEW YORK, NY-01234

Mail Inquiries To:
CUSTOMER SERVICE
PO BOX 1010, TAMPA, FL 30136-3211

Questions?
Call Customer Service: 800-123-4567
Lost or Stolen Card: 800-123-4567

Detach the bottom portion and return payment using enclosed envelope to be received no later than 5:00 pm on the due date. Use black ink.

- -

Account Number   xxx-xxxx—9876 7
New Balance
Minimum Payment Due $30.98   8

Amount Enclosed $_____.___

VISA
PO BOX 0000
NEW YORK, NY 00000

Chad A. Pratt
00 Your Street
BROOKLYN NY 00000

1. **Transactions**—This is a list of all the transactions that have occurred since your last statement (payments, purchases, credits, cash advances, and balance transfers). Some credit card companies group them by type of transaction. Others list them by date of transaction by user, if there are different users on the account. Review the list carefully to make sure you recognize all the transactions. This is the section of your

statement where you can check for unauthorized transactions or other problems.

2. **Account Information**—This is your available credit (your credit limit minus the amount you owe).

3. **Account Summary**—This is a summary of the transactions on your account (your previous balance, payments, credits, purchases, cash advances, fees, interest charges, and amounts past due). It will also show your new balance.

4. **Payment Information**—This shows the minimum payment amount (the least amount you should pay) and the date your payment is due. It will also show your new balance.

5. **Late-Payment Warning**—This section states any additional fees and higher interest rates that may be charged if your payment is late.

6. **Minimum-Payment Warning**—An estimate of how long it can take to pay off your credit card balance if you make only the minimum payment each month and an estimate of how much you likely will pay total, including interest.

7. **Account Number**—Only the last four digits appear for safety precautions.

8. **Minimum Payment Due**—This is the minimum payment amount (the least amount you should pay).

"You always need to read the fine print on your statement. If you look here," Momma P says, pointing, "your credit card contract charges you a fixed annual percentage rate (APR) of 19 percent. An APR is the yearly interest rate on your credit card's balance. To keep your finances in order, you need to know how to calculate the actual interest you pay on your credit card's balance on a monthly basis. But listen." She looks at him, making sure he is paying attention before she continues. "The important thing I want you to remember is that if you *pay off* your entire balance before the due date or at the end of your billing cycle, you don't pay interest or late fees. You only pay interest on *outstanding balances*."

She puts on her reading glasses and draws the statement closer to her. "Go in the junk drawer and pull out a calculator, pad, and pencil."

While Chad is searching for something to write with, Momma P peers over her glasses to look at Nicole and whispers, "Now this is what you should have taught him before you gave him a credit card."

"Yes, you're right ... but honestly, I couldn't explain it, because I didn't fully understand myself. I always pay my credit card balance on time and in full each month, and I told him to do the same to avoid a negative impact on his credit score," Nicole says in her defense.

"That's understandable. Applied knowledge is power, and when you know better, you have the ability to do better. So hopefully, after I explain and show him how to read and calculate the numbers on his credit card statement, he will begin to put his hard-earned money in a savings account and stop throwing it away on unnecessary fees." Chad returns to the table with pen and paper in hand. Momma P continues. "The credit card company is charging you an APR of 19 percent, and your outstanding balance is $1,549.15." She writes the numbers on the paper.

Chad interrupts, "Yeah, that's the thing. My credit limit is only $1,500. How is it that my balance is over that amount when I pay the minimum every month?"

"Because, look. You have a twenty-five-dollar late fee tacked on. When you pay your bill after the due date, the creditors charge you the late fee. That's why you have to read your contract before signing up for a credit card." She pauses before continuing. "If you continue to pay only the minimum of $30.38, it will take you twenty-two years to pay off the total debt of $1,549.15. I'm going to make a chart and show you how this is calculated.

"Your previous balance was $1,400, and you made a charge of $100 on a book called *Rapping for Dummies,* and then you sent a minimum payment after the due date. The creditors charged you a late fee of twenty-five dollars."

"Wait a minute! Stop the press! Stop the press! You bought a book called *Rapping for Dummies*?" Poppa P asks incredulously.

"Yes," Chad answers.

Poppa P shakes his head. "Did it work?"

"Forget that. Let's not get off topic." Momma P frowns at him.

Ignoring her, Poppa P continues, determined to get the last word in, "If it didn't work, that should tell you something!"

Momma P rolls her eyes. "As I was saying, your previous balance, plus your new charge, plus your late fee, plus the interest rate totaled $1,549.15. That is how you exceeded your credit limit. Normally, creditors charge between 1 and 3 percent of your total outstanding balance to calculate your minimum payment. In your case, they charged you 2 percent, and each month they charge you an APR of 19 percent on your outstanding balance. Now I'm going to show you how next month's bill will be calculated with only a minimum payment.

$1,549.15 x 0.02 percent = $30.98 (minimum due)

$1,549.15 x 0.19 percent (APR) = $294.33 divided by 12 months = $24.53 (interest fees)

$30.98 (minimum payment)

-$24.53 (APR interest fees)

_____

$6.45 (principal)

$1,549.15 – $6.45 = $1,542.70

"Out of the $30.98 you will pay, only $6.45 will go toward your outstanding debt, which is hardly a dent. Your next bill balance will be $1,542.70. And if you continue *paying the minimum,* it will take you twenty-two years to pay that debt off. At the end of twenty-two years, you will have paid an extra $3,783.95 in interest fees, which would be a total of $5,333.10."

Chad looks at the math, stunned beyond belief. "You mean to tell me my debt will go from $1,549.15 to $5,333.10?"

Momma P nods. "Exactly. You would have paid $5,333.10 for sneakers and clothes you will toss aside after a few wears or that will become outdated after a few months."

Chad's Credit Card Balance: $1,549.15

19 Percent APR Debt Summary

Pay Entire Bill: $1,549.15	Pay Minimum
$0.00 interest	274 months (22 years) to pay off. Chad will pay $3,783.95 in interest.

	Month	Entire Payment $1,549.15	Interest Paid	Principal Paid	Remaining Balance (Principal)
$1,549.15	1	$1,549.15	$0.00	$1,549.15	$0.00

	Month	Minimum Payment	Interest Rate Paid	Principal Paid	Remaining Balance (Principal)
$	1	$30.98	$24.53	$6.45	$1,542.70
	2	$30.85	$24.43	$6.42	$1,536.28
Minimum Payments Only	3	$30.73	$24.32	$6.41	$1,529.87
	4	$30.59	$24.22	$6.37	$1,523.50

Momma P continues, "Financial institutions are businesses. Their job is to make money. They make money by charging the borrowers' interest fees. Our job is to keep as much money as possible in our pockets. The money you're throwing away to fees decreases the amount you could be saving in the bank, and it lessens your chances of building wealth and reaching your future goals. Why give your hard-earned money away, sinking yourself into poverty while making the people in charge of these companies wealthier?"

"Since you put it like that, it makes me mad just thinking about how I'm giving my money away so they can buy fancy houses, go on fancy trips, and buy fancy cars while I'm riding the iron horse," Chad retorts.

"Okay, that's good," Poppa P cuts in, shaking his head. "Now let that feeling of anger propel you to do better. Around here, buying *Rapping for Dummies* ... um ... um ... um ..."

Momma P interjects, "Let me tell you something, young man, before you get all huffy with financial institutions. Credit and credit cards can either be your friend or your foe, your worst nightmare or your best dream—it depends on how you use them. Credit has the power to help you build wealth, become an entrepreneur, and conquer any dreams you can imagine. If you have no respect for credit, it will turn into your worst nightmare and bring along predators who will attack your entire financial state." Chad is lost in his thoughts, dwelling on his experiences in the last few months.

Letting out a sigh, Chad says, "But looking at my debt, I may not have a choice but to pay $3,783.95 extra in interest fees. I can pay only the minimum. I'm never going to be able to pay this off."

Momma P says softly, "Baby, there's a solution to *every* problem. You must *believe* and *claim* that you *will* pay your debt in full. I want you to repeat after me. 'I Am, who is in me, knows no boundaries.'"

Chad is reluctant.

"Boy, didn't your grandma say repeat after her? Whatcha waiting for? Make it into a rap song or something," says Poppa P, who starts drumming a beat on the table and making funny bebop sounds with his mouth.

"I Am! Who is in me! Knows no boun-da-ries! Knows no boun-da-ries!"

After Chad and Poppa P's performance, Momma P continues, "You have choices. Look at the chart I made for you. There are plenty of options if you are disciplined enough to follow through. Look at options C and D. If you don't make any more charges and pay one hundred fifty or two hundred dollars a month, you will be free of your debt in no time."

Chad looks at the chart and decides that one hundred fifty dollars or a little more every month is doable. Interrupting his thoughts, Momma P says, "Anytime you get a credit card, don't use the entire credit limit. Create your own max by using only a third of the credit limit. Simply put, divide your credit limit by three and make a new limit for yourself. Going forward, after you've paid this debt, don't go over five hundred dollars. That's one of the factors used when your

FICO score is calculated: the amount owed compared to the total credit limit on the card. Poor credit habits affect your score."

"I know, Momma P. My mother already told me about FICO scores."

"Shut up, boy, and stop interrupting grown folks," Poppa P says. "If she wants to tell you again, just keep quiet and listen. Repetition is power. The more it's repeated to you, the more it will become glued to your memory."

Momma P smiles at Poppa P and gives him a wink before continuing. "A FICO is established by the Fair Isaac Corporation. It's a score that breaks down your credit history to a three-digit number that instantly tells a lender whether you are capable of repaying the money you want to borrow. Look, let me show you." She draws a pie chart.

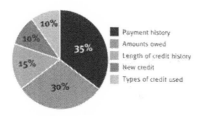

"Your score is determined by your payment history, how much you owe compared to how much you originally borrowed, how long you've had credit, what types of credit you have, and new credit applications. Past payment history and outstanding debt are the two biggest factors in calculating a FICO score. If you consistently make payments after the due date and are using a large percentage of the credit available to you, it affects your FICO number negatively." She turns to face Chad. "Did your mother explain how a low FICO number can have a negative effect on your buying ability, like a cell phone or getting certain jobs, a car, renting an apartment, buying a house, and becoming an entrepreneur?" Chad affirms it with a nod of his head.

Poppa P says, "Good. Make sure you remember those numbers, because we don't want any problems when it's time for you to leave the nest. We already have your father and mother here."

They all ignore Poppa P. Momma P continues, "That's why it's important to stay current on all your bills. The banks charge you an interest rate, depending on your credit history. So if you pay your bills late or not at all, you are considered a risk, and they will charge you a higher interest rate, which is their fee for loaning you money."

"So let me get this straight," Chad says. "Anytime someone borrows money from a bank, they are going to charge the customer a fee for borrowing their money."

Momma P ends with, "Yes. I want you to remember this. Banks are a business. They sell money and other services."

Chad feels a sense of relief now that everything he's been withholding is out in the open and the mystery is solved. He realizes it wasn't the credit card company that was out to get him; the fault lay in his lack of knowledge, misguided decisions, and actions. His actions activated his nightmares too. After his last dream of helping the couple improve their credit, he noticed a feeling of satisfaction, self-fulfillment, and importance. He came to the realization that he liked helping people, particularly with their personal finances. One day he would like to own a financial service or an accounting business.

Taking action toward his vision, he visits with the guidance counselor and discusses the major he plans to pursue in college. He also says to his counselor, "If the offer still stands, I would like to help out in the community center, assisting other students with the college process. I figured out how to adjust my time at work, so it won't interfere with my schoolwork or volunteering."

His counselor is elated. "That's great!" With a curious look, he asks, "What made you change your mind?"

"Let's just say ... I was doused with a wake-up call."

Chad has only one more thing to do: withdraw from the competition. He loves hip-hop—that will never change—but he knows he was pursuing that world for the wrong reasons, reasons that would've left him feeling depleted and unfulfilled. He now understands that he can't measure success by material things or base it on other people's definition of it. Success is based on inner fulfillment.

He plans to continue writing poetry but not as a rapper, only as a guy who likes and enjoys writing poetry. He plans on talking with Jay about collaboration. He would write for his best friend if Jay was interested in using some of his poetry for performances. If not, he has another idea up his sleeve.

He has a serious talk with Melissa and brings her up to speed with his plans on how he's going to attack his credit card bill. She is supportive and stands true to her word. After landing a job and receiving her first paycheck, she starts making contributions toward his bill. He teaches Melissa everything he knows about FICO scores, checking accounts, credit cards, and how to use them responsibly to avoid activating the financial predators who are lurking and waiting to damage whatever future dreams she envisions. He wants to help save Melissa's future dreams from the financial horrors that are sure to appear if she doesn't change her way of thinking.

Surprisingly, she is receptive and interested, which makes him feel a closer connection to her. With the help of her dad, she opens up a student checking and savings account at a neighborhood bank. She is proud to have her own student savings account and begins saving money immediately. Her initial long-term goal was to save for breast implants. By the time she came of age, she figured she would have enough saved up. But as time went on, that goal became less important. She finally accepted what she was born with. With concerted focus and discipline, both Chad and Melissa create successful budget plans for their earned income.

Chad and Melissa have just finished watching a superhero movie. As they exit the dark theater, they discuss the story line and adventures of the main character.

Chad says, "I know this may sound silly, but I felt a connection with the hero of the movie. I feel like a superhero coming to the aid of others each time I help a student at the community center with the college process. I would really love to help others with their personal finances, rescuing their dreams and even helping them create some new ones."

Melissa smiles. "No, it doesn't sound silly. You can start by being *my* superhero." She squirms uncomfortably. Even though Melissa is confident about her relationship with Chad, she's still threatened by Addison.

"Wait," Melissa says, stopping them both in their tracks. "Before we leave, show me or, better yet, introduce me to Addison."

Chad says smoothly, "Another time. I promise."

"Oh … okay." Melissa sighs. *Finally! Can't wait*, she muses.

Feeling a sense of relief and being light at heart, Melissa takes Chad's arm and pulls him toward the exit.

As they walk off, Addison thinks, *Jay Z and Beyoncé don't have nothin' on us.*

Dear Chad:
Your debt is paid in full.

Financially Yours,

M.S. Fee

THE END!

EPILOGUE

Chad continues to teach Melissa everything he learns. Below is a glossary of the financial terms he shares with her.

Glossary

- **account balance**—The dollar value of your savings or checking account. It changes constantly as deposits and sometimes interest earnings are added and as debits, including payments, withdrawals, fees, and other charges, are subtracted.

- **annual fee**—A yearly charge for using a credit card. Not all credit cards have an annual fee, but many premium or reward cards do.

- **annual percentage rate (APR)**—Yearly rate of interest calculated by multiplying the monthly interest rate by twelve (number of months in a year)

- **available credit**—The total amount you can borrow with a revolving credit arrangement, such as a credit card. Amounts you borrow reduce your available credit.

- **borrower**—Also called a "debtor," this person owes money, which he or she promises to repay, plus a finance charge, to the lender

- **budget**—A written plan for managing your income and

expenses to avoid debt

- **checking account**—A transaction account with a bank or a credit union that allows you to transfer money from your account to another account of your choosing (using either a paper check or an electronic funds transfer)

- **credit card**—A payment card issued to users (cardholders) as a method of payment. It allows the cardholder to pay for goods and services based on the holder's promise to pay the lender back at a later date. The issuer of the card (usually a bank) creates a revolving account and grants a line of credit to the cardholder, from which the cardholder can borrow money for payment to a merchant or as a cash advance.

- **credit history**—A record of all the ways you have used credit over the past seven years, including your repayment habits, the amounts you've borrowed, and the types of credit you have applied for or used

- **credit limit**—The most you can borrow with a revolving credit arrangement like a credit card or line of credit. The card issuer or lender sets your credit limit.

- **credit report**—A report detailing an individual's credit history, including payments related to bills, loans, credit accounts and bankruptcies. This information is used to determine one's creditworthiness.

- **credit score**—A three-digit number that represents your creditworthiness based on the information in your credit report

- **creditworthy**—The reputation a borrower establishes for using credit responsibly (in large part by using credit regularly and repaying what is owed on time)

- **debts**—Amounts a borrower owes a lender. Loans and credit card balances are debts.

- **direct deposit**—An electronic funds transfer, in which money is credited to your checking or savings account or divided between them on either a recurring—in case of a paycheck—or an occasional basis.

- **discretionary expenses**—Money a person chooses to spend like money for movies, restaurants, and entertainment. It includes the money you save.

- **down payment**—The amount a lender may require you to pay in cash to be eligible for a loan. Down payments are commonly required when you are buying a home or a car, and are often 10 to 20 percent of the purchase price. The larger your down payment, the less you have to borrow.

- **FAFSA**—Free Application for Federal Student Aid. This is a form the government requires to apply to any federal education aid program. The Free Application for Federal Student Aid is used to determine the expected family contribution based on family financial status.

- **FICA**—An acronym for the Federal Insurance Contribution Act, which authorized the collection of the social security tax, beginning in 1937, and the Medicare tax, beginning in 1966.

- **FICO score**—Created by the Fair Isaac Corporation, this is a way to measure an individual's creditworthiness. A FICO score is a quantification of a variety of factors in an individual's background, including a history of default, the current amount of debt, and the length of time the individual has made purchases on credit. A FICO score ranges between 350 and 850. In general, a score of 650 is considered a "fair" credit score, while 750 or higher is considered "excellent." A FICO score is a convenient way to summarize an individual's credit history and is included in a credit report.

- **finance charge**—Any fee representing the cost of credit or the cost of borrowing. It is interest accrued on, and fees charged for, some forms of credit. It includes not only interest but also other charges, such as financial transaction fees.

- **financial institutions**—Entities that include banks and credit unions that provide financial services to clients. Other examples are insurance companies, brokerage firms, and investment companies.

- **fixed expense**—Expenses that occur regularly and don't change from month to month. Examples of fixed expenses are rent and car payments.

- **fixed interest rate**—Interest rate that stays the same over the course of the loan.

- **flexible expense**—Like fixed expenses, flexible expenses occur on a regular basis. The difference is that with flexible expenses, you have some control over how much you spend. Examples of flexible expenses include food and gasoline.

- **interest**—Money the borrower pays to the lender for the use of the lender's money.

- **interest rate**—The percentage of principal you (1) pay to borrow or (2) earn on deposits in a bank balance or the principal of a debt investment.

- **late fee**—The fee charged when your payment is received after the due date or with some loans after the payment grace period. When you have a balance on your credit card, your payment is due a minimum of twenty-one days after the end of your billing cycle. If you make a payment after your due date or make less than the minimum payment, you'll be charged a late fee.

- **legacy**—Transferable possessions or qualities.

- **minimum payment**—The smallest amount of money customers are permitted to pay each month toward their credit card balance without incurring fees or triggering negative marks on their credit history. For example, if you owe $500 in outstanding charges on your credit card and your minimum payment is $25, you'll have to pay at least that $25 by your bill's due date. If you don't, you'll likely get hit with a late fee, and eventually failure to pay will be reported to the credit bureaus.

- **principal**—The amount you save, invest, or borrow. This is the original borrowed amount. When you save or invest, earnings are calculated as a percentage of the principal. When you borrow, the interest you owe is calculated as a percentage of the principal.
- **savings**—Money you deposit in an insured bank or credit union account for the future rather than spending in the present
- **savings account**—A deposit account at a bank or credit union that allows you to make deposits or take withdrawals but not transfer money to any account that's not held in your own name. In most cases, you earn interest on the principal in the account. There are federal rules that regulate the number of transfers or withdrawals you may make monthly from your savings account.
- **social security**—A federal insurance program that provides benefits to retired people and those unemployed or disabled
- **variable interest rate**—The interest rate can change over the course of a loan.
- **volunteering**—Generally considered a self-sacrificing activity, where an individual or group provides services for no financial gain. Volunteering is also intended to promote goodness or to improve human quality of life. Volunteering may have positive benefits for the volunteer and for the person or community served. .

Sources

- https://www.bankrate.com/
- https://studentaid.gov/h/apply-for-aid/fafsa
- https://studentaid.gov/understand-aid/types/loans

WORKBOOK: TEACHER'S GUIDE - GUIDED READING QUESTIONS FOR CLASS DISCUSSION

Self-Honesty

- Would Chad have been happy as a rapper? Why or why not?
- Do you think Poppa P was being mean or helpful?
- What outside influences affected Chad's decision to want to be a rapper?
- Chad was in financial turmoil and trying to understand the fees accumulating on his credit card statement. Do you feel his problem could have been solved much sooner? If so, how?
- Now that Chad has been taught the aspects of personal finance, do you think he will be a good manager of his money and credit? If not, who is to blame and why?
- Chad has the potential of having a bright financial future; what obstacles could hold Chad back from reaching his dreams?

Integrity

Integrity means doing the right thing when nobody is watching.
- How does Chad illustrate integrity? Give an example.
- Do you agree with Melissa when she suggested Chad not pay his dad back? Why or why not?
- Have you ever been afraid to be honest about something?

Respecting Others

- Do you think Chad's manager was overbearing?
- Did the manager help or hinder Chad?
- What does his manager mean when he tells Chad, "Time is money"?
- What does it mean to "take personal responsibility" for something?
- Give an example of a situation where you have taken responsibility for making sure something got done.
- Have you ever borrowed money from someone? What kind of agreement did you make with him or her about paying the money back? Did you keep your promise?
- Have you ever loaned money to someone? What was the agreement?

Legacy

Legacy is a transferable quality.
- What do you want your legacy to be?
- Are you living your legacy now?
- How do you want to be remembered?
- What changes would you like to see in the world?
- What do you value most?
- Do your spending and giving reflect your values?

Believing in Yourself

- Momma P compares life to a puzzle. What does that mean?
- Do you feel and know you have what it takes to succeed in life?
- What is an affirmation?
- Is it important to repeat affirmations?
- What affirmation does Momma P tell Chad to repeat?

Addison

- Who is Addison, and what is Chad and Addison relationship?
- Why does Chad keep Addison a secret from Melissa?

Nightmares

- How are Chad's nightmares related, and what relevant actions illustrate Chad's growth?
- Do you think Chad created his own nightmares? If so, how?
- In the beginning, Chad's first nightmare included a man in a gray suit reaching out to save him. Ironically, in his last nightmare Chad is dressed the same way as the man in the first nightmare. What could that similarity symbolize?
- What financial habits can Chad develop to set himself up for success?

UNDERSTANDING CHAD'S CREDIT CARD STATEMENT

----

1. If Chad chooses to pay the minimum every month, how long will it take to pay off the entire credit? (See Chapter 14)
   a. 10 years
   b. 22 years
   c. 24 months

2. If Chad continues to make late payments or doesn't pay at all, what will happen?

Explain Chad's Credit Card Statement
(see Chapter 14)

1. Transactions:
   What store did Chad shop in?
   On what date did he make his purchases?

2. Account Information:
   How much is Chad 's available credit? What is Chad 's credit limit?

3. Account Summary:
   What is Chad 's balance?

4. Payment Information:
   What is the minimum payment due?

5. Late-Payment Warning:
   What is Chad 's late-fee amount?

6. Late and Minimum Payment Warning:
   What does it say on Chad 's credit card statement?

7. Account Number:
   What is the last 4 numbers of Chad 's account number?

8. Minimum Payment Due:
   When is Chad 's minimum payment due?

Give Me Some Credit!

Based on what you've learned from Chad's experience, mark each of the following statements True (**T**) or False (**F**).

1. You don't ever have to pay back a credit card. _____

2. Your credit rating will be better if you pay your bills on time. _____

3. It's smart to always charge items on your credit card. _____

4. An emergency is a good time to use a credit card. _____

5. Once you get a credit card, you should buy anything you want. _____

6. Your credit limit is the amount of money you can spend on your credit card. _____

If you are turned down for credit because your score is too low, how can you improve it? Put a "T" by the statements you think are true and a "F" by the statements you think are false.

1. Stop using your credit cards and just pay cash. _____

2. Use a credit card every month and pay at least the minimum due on time. _____

3. Check your credit report for errors and request that any errors be corrected. _____

Using "1" to indicate the most important and "5" to indicate the least important, rank the factors that determine your credit score. (See Chapter 7)

A. _____ Types of credit you've used

B. _____ Length of your credit history

C. _____ Outstanding balances in relation to your available credit

D. _____ Payment history, including repayment of student loans

E. _____ Number of inquiries or new accounts you've opened

Answer Page

Understanding Chad's Credit Card Statement

1. If Chad chooses to pay the minimum every month, how long will it take to pay off the entire credit balance?

   Answer: b. 22 years.

2. If Chad continues to make late payments or doesn't pay his bill at all, what will happen?

   Answer: He will have to pay late fees. Late fees will negatively impact his credit score.

Explain Chad's Credit Card Statement

1. Bookstore. The purchase was made on November 10th.

2. $0.00. Credit limit is $1,500.

3. $1,549.15.

4. $30.98.

5. $25.

6. Late-Payment Warning: If we do not receive your minimum payment by the date listed above, you may have to pay a $25 late fee. Minimum-Payment Warning: If you make only the minimum payment each period, you will pay more in interest, and it will take you longer to pay off your balance. The table is based on your standard minimum payment and does not include any past-due and over-limit amounts.

7. xxx-9876.

8. January 12th.

Lisa McCorkle

Give Me Some Credit!

Based on what you've learned from Chad's experience, mark each of the following statements True (**T**) or False (**F**).

1. You don't ever have to pay back a credit card. **F**
2. Your credit rating will be better if you pay your bills on time. **T**
3. It's smart to always charge items on your credit card. **F**
4. An emergency is a good time to use a credit card. **T**
5. Once you get a credit card, you should buy anything you want. **F**
6. Your credit limit is the amount of money you can spend on your credit card. **T**

If you are turned down for credit because your score is too low, how can you improve it? Put a "**T**" by statements you think are true and an "**F**" by statements you think are false.

1. Stop using your credit cards and just pay cash. **F**

   You must show you can use credit wisely to improve your score.

2. Use a credit card every month and pay at least the minimum due on time. **T**

   This practice demonstrates a responsible use of credit.

3. Check your credit report for errors and request that any errors be corrected. **T**

   This is a good idea even if you haven't been turned down for credit.

Using "1" to indicate the most important and "5" to indicate the least important, rank the factors that determine your credit score.

A. <u>5</u> Types of credit you've used.

B. <u>3</u> Length of your credit history.

C. <u>2</u> Outstanding balances in relation to your available credit.

D. <u>1</u> Payment history, including repayment of student loans.

E. <u>4</u> Number of inquiries or new accounts you've opened.

Let me know what you think about THE BATTLE OF FINANCE AND FAME. For speaking requests, book signings, contact:

financeisfame@gmail.com

Follow me on Instagram @financeisfame

FinanceisF.A.M.E (Freedom, Assets, Mindfulness, Empowerment)

Books Make Great Gifts! THE BATTLE OF FINANCE AND FAME, A Financial Novel and Guide for teenagers is a great gift for teenagers, parents, grandparents'. Finance is essential, everyone can relate to personal finance/money.

Made in the USA
Coppell, TX
13 December 2022

89126805R00090